Calcu
on Your
Plate

Nilosree Biswas is an author and filmmaker trained in comparative literature and later in cinema. She writes about history (often colonial Bengal and pre-modern India), culture, art history, food and cinema of South Asia. These areas of interests extend to her frequent national and international columns.

Her earlier books include *Banaras: Of Gods, Humans and Stories* and *Alluring Kashmir: The Inner Spirit* (co-written with Irfan Nabi).

Two decades of film work has earned Nilosree awards like the 'Best Documentary' in the New York Festival, with documentaries showcased at the Cannes Film Festival and archived by the Academy of Motion Picture Arts and Sciences (Oscar), Los Angeles.

She is currently working on her next book with themes related to colonial Bengal.

Calcutta
on Your
Plate

Nilosree Biswas
Photographs by **Irfan Nabi**

RUPA

Published by
Rupa Publications India Pvt. Ltd 2022
7/16, Ansari Road, Daryaganj
New Delhi 110002

Sales centres:
Allahabad Bengaluru Chennai
Hyderabad Jaipur Kathmandu
Kolkata Mumbai

P-ISBN: 978-93-5520-774-6
E-ISBN-978-93-5520-775-3

First impression 2022

10 9 8 7 6 5 4 3 2 1

The moral right of the author has been asserted.

Printed in India

For

Prof. Subir Ray Chowdhury
Zaitoon Khan
Renu Ghosh Dastidar
Subarna Rani Biswas
&
Calcutta and its street-food vendors
—Nilosree Biswas

For
Zaitoon Khan
&
Mummy, I love you more than ever and
will meet you again on the other side
—Irfan Nabi

Contents

Introduction

*S*ometimes, seemingly disjointed incidents, fictitious or real, are interconnected, though their occurrences could be marked by a gap of centuries or more.

In such a canvas of time fit the following anecdotes that would mostly help us put together the story of gastronomy—its influences, rejections, encounters, acceptances and celebrations of nearly a 340-year-old city now known as Kolkata (erstwhile Calcutta and even earlier as Sutanati, Gobindopur and Dihi Kolikatah).

Tracing where it all began is not quite possible; however, to create a narrative about Bengali food, one needs to go back and forth—almost in a cinematic style of storytelling, which would have several cognizant elements: some frivolous, others painstakingly traced lost tales. This together would help build a complex discourse on edibles of Kolkata.

Cross-pollinated by a plethora of influences, Kolkata's food can be defined as unique, hybrid and inclusive. To attain this definition, the city took more than 200 years, by the end of which, its food culture could be read as an amalgam of love for food, invented recipes and fascinating anecdotes of culinary indulgences, sometimes restraint, sprinkled with social history. The city's gastronomy is not a defined story of an ethnicity's interest in culinary delights but rather an exploration into the psyche of a community that has made their love for food a statement of self-expression, a desirous open secret like no other!

LITTLE BY LITTLE

In the mid-sixteenth century, around 1545–47, Mukundaram Chakraborty, a Bengali littérateur who used the nom de plume 'Kabikankan', describes the everyday life of a hunter couple who sells their proceeds from the hunt in the nearby villages in exchange of their daily provisions, in his medieval eulogy literature *Chandimangal Kabyo*[1]. The text, written in a poetic form, eloquently depicts a modest but tough life of lower-caste hunters. Phullara, the wife, describes Bengali food habits in what is one of the vivid testimonies ever written in a medieval text. In the novella, the segment is titled 'Phullarar's Baromashya' (Twelve Months of Phullara's Life) and grippingly reveals a picture of food availability—farmed as well as wild produces.

The story concludes with Goddess Chandi relieving Phullara and her husband Kalketu of their abject poverty, blessing them with a reversal of fortune filled with abundance. It is rather interesting how from the times of the *Mangal Kabyos*, the food angle has remained a constant in Bengali storytelling.

One of the plausible reasons for this omnipresent mention of eatables in literary works was Bengal's endowed geography, which produced rich yields of rice, fresh fish, vegetables and abundant milk. How this advantage of fertile land and robust rivers was transformed into artful expressions of culinary experiments, the desire for a good life and a passion unmatched—almost bordering obsession—is indeed a fascinating story.

In 1608, Emperor Jahangir, via Maharaja Man Singh, his viceroy in Bengal, handed over the jagirdari of a vast tract of land in southern Bengal to a local zamindar named Lakshmikant Gangopadhyay, conferring on him the titles of 'Ray' and 'Chowdhury', which he readily took up.

Within their territory of mosquito-infested marshy tracts, criss-crossed with a network of rivers, were three villages, namely Sutanati, Gobindopur and Kolikatah. We find mention of Kolikatah as one of these three indiscrete villages in a letter written to Job Charnock, an agent of the East India Company

(EIC), by Sir Charles Eyre, an administrator of the British EIC and founder of Fort William. It is to Charnock that the city's foundation is credited by most and to whose eldest daughter Sir Charles would be later married.

The rise of the first imperial capital of India is intertwined with the EIC's clever and often aggressive business strategies. While the English contributed to the urban development of this sprawling city, the same cannot be flaunted about Kolkata's food. The contributors to the city's foodscape were many, including the Portuguese, the Dutch, the Armenians, the Afghans and the Chinese, among others, each bringing their food cultures, ingredients, recipes and techniques of cooking hitherto unknown.

Around the late sixteenth century, the Portuguese produced a variety of cheese (both fresh and aged), pickles and condiments at their settlements in Bandel, Cossimbazar and Hooghly. Their fresh cheese influenced the birth of chhana or casein, the staple ingredient in roshogolla and sandesh, the ubiquitous sweets originating in Bengal.

The petite refreshment room at Eden Gardens started in 1840. It was lovingly designed by Governor General Lord Auckland's sister Emily Eden, a sweet spot that ushered in a trend of all-day snacking and afternoon teas—a pastime that was dear to the English.

Nawab Wajid Ali Shah, the last king of Awadh, arrived at Calcutta from Awadh–Lucknow by a quirk of fate on 6 May 1856 in a steamer called *General McLeod*, on his way to London, where he was supposed to meet the Queen of England. With him came his retinue of *bawarchis* (cooks), *rakabdars* and *khansamas* (gourmet chefs), and the phenomenal Awadhi cuisine.

Peliti's Restaurant at 11 Government Place, owned by Federico Peliti—an Italian baker, confectioner, hotelier and photographer—was already famed. His other restaurant in Simla too was already famous and the hill town's crème de la crème would throng there for their daily dose of tea, cakes and gossip. The outlet at Government Place opened its doors to the public in 1870 and a three-course lunch—the sole reason for an Englishman's day out—would cost 1 rupee 50 paisa.

Fascinatingly, these are no random nuggets of cultural history. In contrast, they are game changers, happenings through which Calcutta's gastronomy slowly emerged. A universe in itself, laced with worldly desires of its players, lusting an indulgent existence. Such an existence, in turn, was intrinsically linked with the lives of the bhadraloks (literally 'gentlemen'), who were just starting to see things differently. Here was the emergence of a stratum within the larger community—the elite Bengalis, with a furious passion for food, an element they also used for self-fashioning, for identifying themselves. By the late eighteenth century, European lifestyle was starting to make a deep incision in the everyday living of the Bengali bhadraloks. They nurtured their fancy for a highly anglicized luxurious life. Food became their primal expression.

The EIC's presence led to the growth of the city, starting with a huge fort being built on the banks of the river Hooghly. As more men got employed by the Company, many of them started feeling homesick. They hoped to live 'their' kind of life that included familiar food, social circle and entertainment, which would then keep them going. They decided to transform Calcutta into London of the East and thus began the process of recreation.

Interesting observations by contemporary travellers sum

up how the city appeared to a passing visitor, reaffirming this metamorphosis. Famed French photographer and traveller Louis Rousselet, who visited India through 1864 and 1868, extending his six months of planned trip to years, does not mince his words, 'I shall not speak of life which Europeans led in Calcutta. With the upper English classes, it is only a copy of high life in London; they dance, dine, drink tea.'[2] Rousselet creates an intriguingly fascinating visual imagery of English and European life at large. In reality, too, a lot was happening in Calcutta.

The wealthy landed gentry swarmed to burgeoning Calcutta like droves of bees to a beehive. Everyone wanted to be seen in the British social circle. Many of these zamindars had a good life of unlimited food and wine accompanied by amorous pursuits. With English influences, they now nurtured a dream of becoming baboos.

Baboo (or varyingly spelt as Babu) is a generic term used for the affluent upper class that was integral to the changing cultural face of this infant city. They were high on life, competing with each other in their display of social clout. In no time, free-flowing, imported alcohol, stunning nautch performances and delectable food prepared by bawarchis and rakabdars became the signature of a fine baboo, a connoisseur. In their private kitchens, the bawarchis and rakabdars created a well-defined cuisine, based on their familial knowledge as well as what their employers craved for, as they went berserk in entertaining the Europeans. The firangs, who were passionately fond of their meat and confectionaries, helped introduce meat cooking and baking in these upwardly mobile households.

These were days when baboos like the Debs, the Rays, the Mullicks, the Bysaks, the Deys and the Mitras were increasingly gaining power in the social ecology of the city. Their kitchens churned out dishes earlier unheard of: roast chicken, mutton cutlet, steak and kidney pie, and bread pudding. The clever and fearless baboos first introduced poultry as a lesser evil, as a milder variety of meat, followed by mutton and lamb. Platters of roasts, grills and a variety of kebabs made their way to Bengali dining tables. The sweet dishes shielded the baboos from harsh criticism by themselves. Consequently, English puddings, teacakes and custards found their place in the kitchens of some such households.

The baboos' obsession with socializing compelled the English press of Calcutta to write about these lavish parties, which also held nautch performances, accompanied by unrestrained food and alcohol.

The Europeans, by and large, can be given the credit of initiating a sea change in Bengali cuisine. The colonizers introduced a long list of ingredients such as chicken, potatoes, tomatoes, green chillies, papaya, okra, cilantro (coriander), pineapple, peach, guava, strawberry, cashews and more, as well as new cooking techniques and recipes. Meanwhile, the English got their brownie points by introducing eggs in its many avatars—from the fluffy omelette to the often-mispronounced mumlet, a desi version of the omelette, made with copious amounts of chopped green chillies and fried in mustard oil. Then there was the bright sunny side up egg poach in a classical combo of mildly toasted slices of bread topped with a creamy spread of butter. They also introduced a typical chicken curry, cutlets and chops. And most indispensably, came cha or tea with biskut (the Bengali way of pronouncing 'biscuit'). Soon, cha would become a blockbuster brew.

The Portuguese influences are much fewer than their

English counterparts and include many of the vegetables mentioned earlier, most importantly the ubiquitous potatoes, green chillies and tomatoes. However, the undeniable and most distinct Portuguese contribution is the technique of making fresh cottage cheese or chhana. A traditional Hindu sweet maker did not know the use of chhana in parlance to sweetmeat making before the seventeenth century. Accidental curdling of milk till recently was not a happy thing at Hindu Bengali kitchens. Portuguese settlers inspired and influenced Bengali moiras, or sweetmeat makers, to experiment with breaking of milk by using whey, and thus chhana—a close cousin of the Portuguese cottage cheese *queijo fresco*—was born. This became the base material of the quintessential roshogolla by Nobin Chandra Das, a Bengali confectioner, in 1868 and the delectable sandesh by Bhim Nag, and Girish Chandra Dey & Nakur Chandra Nandy.

Chhana was to stay forever as the key ingredient of Bengali sweetmeats. The Portuguese even named one of their cottage cheese 'Bandel', a namesake of their settlement in the Hooghly district. Chhana was the highlight of Portuguese influence that led to the rise of an enormous sweetmeat culture in Bengal in the next hundred years.

A lot was happening in the social circle of Calcutta in the nineteenth century and yet all seems profane in comparison to the happenings that took place in and around the address 11 Garden Reach. Here lived the last king of colonized India, Nawab Wajid Ali Shah, a tenant of the Maharaja of Burdwan, Chand Mehtab Bahadur, for a rent of ₹500 a month. How instrumental the Nawab was in reinventing the foodscape of Calcutta will follow later in the book, but to understand his love for good food, it is critical to know him and the last

30 years of his life, while he was exiled in Garden Reach.

The Nawab wanted to replicate Lucknow and in bargain, Calcutta got more than what it could have ever imagined. His personal rakabdars, khansamas and bawarchis, who had joined the rushed entourage that Wajid Ali Shah took in 1856 as he headed to London, were the key players in retaining the culinary culture of Awadh. The detour that was forced upon him after he was imprisoned in Fort William by the British brought the entire population to Metiaburj (meaning, a fortress made of clay) or present-day Garden Reach area. The scale of happenings is rather indescribable, but in just two years from his arrival, an estimated 300 households grew around 11 Garden Reach, with the mansion he lived in renamed Sultan Khana. In here, at the Nawab's royal kitchen, the art of cooking continued which eventually percolated into the public domain, destined to be immortalized. The Nawab, who identified himself as a man of refined tastes, which indeed he was, introduced Calcutta to the technique of dum (cooking on slow fire), and the use of yogurt in meat and fish preparations, along with the induction of aromatic spices, primarily saffron and cardamom.

What the city has embraced as its identity today: the scrumptious biryani, with its signature chunky piece of boiled potato, the delectable rezala, and many kebabs and kathi rolls are all contributions of Wajid Ali Shah and his amazing band of chefs, who after his demise, found employment of some stature with the dak bungalows and English Clubs and even later at upcoming hotels of the city, some going on to become head cooks. Some even started their own ventures.

To a good extent, initially, all this was about self-fashioning, about being in the good books of the colonial rulers and leading an extravagant life. With time, merely appropriating British lifestyle was not what the Bengali baboos and bhadraloks were looking at. They were open to culinary experiments, welcoming unfamiliar ingredients, trying out new recipes and techniques. At the core of this was building a new culinary identity, deeply associated with self-pride and innovations, resulting in amazing inventions like the roshogolla, ledikeni (an oblong deep-fried sweet in sugar syrup) and a whole universe of sandesh. Other such experiments included the fowl curry, which metamorphosed into the quintessential Bengali chicken curry, chicken jalfrezi, kabiraji (a mutton cutlet variant coated with a fluffy egg batter and egg mesh), deemer devil (scotched eggs), telebhajas (deep fries), and more.

This book tells the story of Calcutta's food, the platter that is identified as the city's grub as well as the notion of *amader khabar* (our eats) as I situate Bengali gastronomy. The narrative does not follow a year-by-year account of changes that Bengali food has undergone, because no gastronomic history is chronological. Going back and forth, I explore how multifarious factors played their part in creating food tastes, leading to choices. Timelines are therefore of secondary importance, but the winning factor is attributed to the agencies of change.

How present-day Kolkata evolved as the new trading post of the Company, the life of its locals as well as the foreigners who settled in lieu of employment or trade, and finally its growth as an urban centre, sets this story. Interestingly, many don't know Calcutta as a pre-colonial entity. A seventh-century annal by the Hindu astronomer Varahamihira (also called Varaha or Mihira) has a one-off mention of the current location of the city and its adjoining areas as hills of alluvial mounds. A.K. Ray, the city's surveyor, in 1901, includes this geomorphic description as part of Calcutta's earliest-known history. He mentions a Sanskrit word *'samatata'* (meaning, a tidal swamp) in the antiquarian text.[3]

Kalighat, a religious spot even today, has also been linked with pre-colonial Calcutta. The location found its mention in the oft-quoted Hindu mythology of Sati and Shiva, where the former's body parts were strewn all over the world. And it is said that one of those parts fell on the same site where the Kalighat Temple stands today. *Manashamangal Kabyo,* a medieval Bengali text, bears another prominent mention of Calcutta. Chand Saudagar, the protagonist, is a prosperous merchant who travels past these tidal swamps as he sails through the river Hooghly, heading to the Bay of Bengal. The lyrical novella refers to the spot as a *Kalikhestra* (site of Goddess Kali). Kalighat was thus a seemingly recognized site of pilgrimage, a more relatable cornerstone to identify pre-colonial Calcutta.

To that there are records of trade activities, making the site reasonably important for business. A.K. Ray, in 'A Short History of Calcutta', writes:

> The old zamindars of Calcutta further claim that it was the hât and bazar round their idols and their pucka zamindari *cutcherry* west of the tank that gave Calcutta its original importance and gave rise to the names of 'Hat tala' (latterly corrupted into 'Hatkhola'), and Burrabazar (Bura being a familiar name of Siva); that it was the dôles near the Kali's temple that attracted a large population and contributed to the reclamation and cultivation of marsh and jungle, and that their culverts, landing ghats and roads, with a shady avenue of trees on their sides formed the only adornment of rural Calcutta in its early days.[4]

While Ray, in the *Census of 1901*, elaborates on both locations—Kalighat and Calcutta, historical records also confirm the presence of a village called Gobindopur, along with a weekly market by the name of Sutanuti Hât around 1550.[5]

Early *haats* (markets) sprouted due to religious tourism germinating around temples, with potential for sale of edible items. It makes me imagine large gathering of locals and travellers on haat days.

Seth and Basak familial traders were the founders of the Sutanati Hât. They made it big even in the local context, much like their businesses with the Portuguese and the Dutch from their Satgaon days. 'They are said to have cleared much jungle, and there is but little doubt that it was chiefly through them that Gobindopur and Sutanati got a large colony of weavers and a flourishing trade in cotton bales in later years, which became an attraction for the English Merchant Company.'[6]

C.R. Wilson further states in *The Early Annals of the English in Bengal*,

> This foreign market attracted native traders and merchants to the spot, and in particular, four families of Bysacks and one of Setts, leaving the then rapidly declining city of Satgaon, came and founded the settlement of Govindpur on the site of the present Fort William, and established the Sutanuti market, on the north side of Calcutta, where they did business with the Portuguese.[7]

Whether these local trading families socialized with the Portuguese at that point is not known, but it is certain that their business was robust. Competition heightened with the EIC eyeing Bengal. However, it would take some more years for the English to clench their teeth into Bengal, but by then, they had secured trades of saltpetre and cotton.

Charnock had big dreams when he landed on the banks of Hooghly. After several skirmishes, Kolkata (erstwhile Calcutta) was founded by the English agent on 24 August 1690. Having founded the city, Charnock realized the need for manpower. This in turn meant more Englishmen travelling from England to Calcutta, settling in the mosquito-infested lower delta of the river.

Imaginably, the idea of replicating London via this muddy village struck Charnock's mind. However, sadly, destiny failed him. He died in 1693, just three years after founding Calcutta, a city that he was growing attached to. But those three years were critical. Charnock found himself on a better ground by being at loggerheads with the governors of Bengal—one of the rarest happenings in the history of imperial India, when a serious animosity between a ruler and a trading agent brought in bigger transformation favouring the agent, not the ruler. Charnock realized that these feuds would eventually lead to better prospect of English trading enabling the Company to profit more and eventually ensure his own position.

With Charnock's death, it got strongly ascertained that Calcutta had an undeniable potential to become the London of the East. Proving the point in the next 200 years or so, the city would be a safe haven for thousands of Englishmen and women, who lived a perfect Londoner life. Replicating London meant recreating an ideal British life and what best than introducing a lifestyle with food being the major crossover between the English, the rest of the Europeans and the wealthy locals.

Calcutta on Your Plate sets the tone with these impressions from the early EIC days, which not only generated revenues from silk and cotton trades but also engineered the building blocks of one of the world's biggest cities. I touch upon how Kolkata looked in its early days, its lived-in spaces. The discussion moves to gastronomy, revolving around the major actors that were instrumental in the emergence of a new food order. Routing via throwback, the book walks the story of early taverns, hotels in the city, dak bungalows and transit food along with stories of what was sold and consumed. There are descriptions of buying trends and how advertisement with quirky wordings titillated the baboos enough to lure them into a redefined luxurious life. Discussions revolve around their outdoor life, discreet sojourns at hotels and travels out of Bengal. All in all, there was a behavioural change in the affluent, educated class of Bengalis, much like their food, and this is one of the central themes throughout the book.

The narrative closely looks into Calcutta life of the eighteenth and nineteenth centuries, when Bengalis were becoming uninhibited, albeit a tad selectively, as many of them got into English education. Soon, women's education would follow, with a handful of all girls' schools opening. Though met with initial resistance, education would act as one of the most influential factors towards the rise of 'new food'. With the advent of the printing press, a whole world of women's magazines surfaced. These magazines fostered discussions on home management and culinary, letting women take a proactive role in penning their stories of food including recipes they came up with. To that, there were manuals written by men, conveying the idea of an ideal Bengali woman and her role at home.

No new food order is created or accepted overnight. What is known as Kolkata's food today has its backstory embedded in

250 years of political, social and cultural history—a fascinating testimony of self-fashioned Bengali baboos, whose aspirations pushed the boundaries of Bengal's traditional gastronomy, resulting in a new food universe.

From the private kitchen of an exiled king and the homes of a handful of upper-class Bengalis, how some dishes became so popular, is a thrilling story of taste, smell and savouring. To think that some of today's signature dishes such as dum biryani, kebabs, fish chops, kabirajis, cutlets, kathi rolls and Mughlai paratha were once exclusive to those who had access to the ingredients or for whom it was their 'home food', is perhaps overwhelming at some level.

With influences of two cooking styles—namely the English and the Mughlai-Awadhi, aided by contributions of the Portuguese and an already pre-existing food habit from the medieval times—Calcutta's foodscape underwent a sea change, impacting people's lives, food habits, food procurement, desires and the ways of social engagement.

And this is what the book touches upon in the following pages.

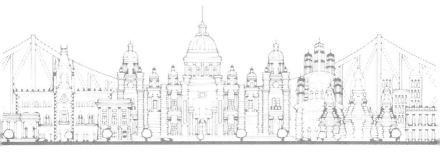

1

Charnock, Muddy Tracts and the Old Cotton Market

One might assume that Kolkata's present food habits and choices happened because Bengali elites of the eighteenth and nineteenth centuries simply chose to live their firangi dream and accept European tastes. However, that really wasn't the case. The city's food habits did not change overnight, nor was it only about curiosity or acceptance of the European platter.

Deeper reasons for this adaptation, I would argue, were not only an act of acculturation but were driven by the business stakes that Bengali men had with the British EIC at large. This was also related to building clout and gaining influence within the decision-makers of the Company or with an Englishman of position.

The decision of the Company officials to settle in Calcutta in August 1690, during the third phase of their business expansion, was a watershed moment, which would lead to cultural appropriations and adaptations for both the English and the locals.

Job Charnock, the EIC agent, was looking for a unique location in southern Bengal—a location that would give him a high hand over his European competitors and certainly over Shaista Khan, the governor. He nurtured interests in the muddy lower basin of the river Hooghly, setting his eyes on Sutanati. Not only was his goal to make English trade in Bengal a monopoly, he also wished and planned for a stable fortified trading station amidst these brackish waters covered with dense forests and inhabited by plenty of perilous animals and infinite mosquitoes.

In 'A Short History of Calcutta', A.K. Ray describes what led Job Charnock to zero in on Calcutta, the future trading post of the EIC.

The days for begging favour at the Viceroy's hands had vanished. The spirit of the peaceful merchant had disappeared. The idea of a footing of equality with the governing Nabob had already gained ground, and the claim for a fort and for coining their own money had been steadily put forward, in spite of the Nabob's active hostility and outspoken threats.[1]

He continues,

Job Charnock had lived at Cassimbazar and left it. He had stayed at Hooghly and given it up. He had seen Balasore and forsaken it. He had resided at Hidgelee and turned away from it. He had tried Uluberia and abandoned it. He had but visited Chuttanutte once before on his way down the Hooghly and had returned to it, a second time. There was something in it that had undoubtedly greater attractions for him than those other places. The Nabob wished him to settle his factory near Hooghly, but Charnock stirred not. He had felt that Chuttanutte had advantages for the English which the others lacked. Provisions were plentiful at its hâts and bazars. There was a broad road for communication by land with the interior, and yet the village was an island and could be cheaply defended. It was a secure position for a naval power.[2]

The area was a thick jungle cover that had tigers, snakes and dacoits, and the population was thin, with hunters, woodcutters and fishermen living on the dihis, or the high spots of the riverside. It was only natural that farming cannot be an occupational practice here, as forests and marshy lands together dominated the landscape, making it uncultivable. Charnock's sharp business acumen knew that reworking the large patch of land would not be difficult. He silently hoped that Sutanati and its adjacent territory would allow him a firm locational base and even become a lucky charm.

Charnock also had pressures to deal with. In the eyes of his bosses, he needed that little tweak or brush of luck that would restore their confidence in him. It did happen, but in a rather roundabout way, when destiny played in. Around 1652, Englishmen James Bridgeman and Edward Stephens were trying their best to negotiate with the local governor, Nawab Shaista Khan, to set up a factory at Hooghly. The negotiations yielded a deal, with a factory at Hooghly and three agencies at Balasore, Cassimbazaar and Patna. Charnock was appointed the fourth in-charge at this factory.

Although the factory was established, rivalries leading to occasional strife with the Portuguese and the Nawab's men continued. 'In 1667, Emperor Aurangzeb granted letters-patent to the English for free trade, and in the year 1668, they established an agency at Dacca, which was the then capital of Bengal. And in 1672, Shayista Khan, Governor of Bengal, proclaimed due adherence to the terms of the grant.'[3]

The first nod from the central court was a huge seal of assurance for the EIC. Food historian Lizzie Collingham mentions, '[The] English East India Company gradually put down their firm roots. The popularity of Indian textiles in Britain shifted the company's focus towards India as the trade in cotton and calicoes began to overtake in spices.'[4] That the EIC was gaining ground was evident from how trade activities were accentuated in the east of the country. Between 1668 and 1680, the English stock value had a rise from £31,000 to £150,000, with phenomenal growth in the business of saltpetre, sugar and silk.[5] At this point, it might seem that the EIC was finally getting into the good books of the Mughals and the local rulers, but this wasn't the whole picture.

Mughal emperor Aurangzeb had favourable orders for the English, but it was Shaista Khan in Bengal who wasn't easy to deal with. The mutual skirmishes were not one off any more and Charnock's morals were not in high spirits. He was desperate to flourish and consolidate English trade interests in Bengal. At the back of all this, his intent was to create a unique branding for himself, which would give him a better stature, rising up the ladder from being the fourth man in order.

A string of events helped Charnock's cause. Applications with requests for custom-free trade, a large piece of land, enough to build a fort and a mint were sent to Shaista Khan in the winter of 1686–87. Charnock spent a hopeful Christmas, but after waiting for several weeks, the requests were repealed, sighting the Emperor's disapproval. This was not a commonplace incident for the Company or for Charnock. It came as a rude shock. Additionally, the Nawab passed an action plan to drive away the English from Bengal. Without any more possibilities of negotiation in sight, Charnock attacked Hooghly and his men ransacked everything including the Emperor's properties and his salt houses.

To his odd luck, though he ransacked Hooghly, giving Khan's men a tough fight, his bosses in London were not happy. They found his strategies and approaches far too off the mark from the Company's agenda. Hardly did they know the realities on ground. It was Charnock who knew the ground reality, although he was no genius and deep down, knew that too. Soon, much to Charnock's irk, Captain William Heath (better known as Captain Heath), his competitor, was promoted. That Heath could never enhance the interests of the EIC and finally retreated to Madras (now Chennai) is another story. However, Heath's return to Madras surely gave Charnock a chance out of the blue, a wider playground to come back into eminence.

'Charnock, as I have said,' comments C.R. Wilson in *The Early Annals of the English in Bengal*, 'was not a genius to divine by intuition what should be done, but he was a shrewd, clever man, who quickly profited by experience. He had tried three places on the right side of the river, Hugli, Ulubaria, Hijili. The first two were completely exposed to the attack of an enemy—advancing from the west, and it was therefore impossible for the English to remain at either of them if the Mogul Government attacked in sufficient force.'[6]

Charnock took a calculated risk. In 1688, he was back in Sutanati. 'In fact, Charnock had the wisdom to see that a settlement on the banks of the Hugli would be more suitable to the requirements of English trade. Accordingly, after trying Hijuli and finding it too unhealthy, he fixed upon Sutanuti as the best place.'[7] And on a rainy afternoon of 24 August 1690, he set anchor in Hooghly and the city of Calcutta was thus founded.

On the swampy riverside, Charnock initiated a settlement that was to be the seat of British Empire in India and the seed of what would become the London of the Orient. According to Hamilton's *New Account of the East Indies*, 'Mr Charnock choosing the Ground of the Colony, where it now is, reigned more absolute than a Rajah.'

This remark, which historian William Dalrymple refers to in his book *The Anarchy,* harps on Charnock as a character— that he was unique in his thoughts and if not a genius, he was hugely instinctive in his decisions.[8]

The next years would prove Charnock's decision right as the settlement grew on the swampy ground, albeit a tad unplanned but an enviable urban centre nevertheless. Calcutta grew to be the biggest and most prosperous city of imperial India, flourishing on an unthinkable scale, beginning from nowhere but a trading post.

Life in the new-born city was a dazzling mix of European high life and desi, local extravaganza that brought changes in the everyday living of Bengali elites and some amongst the English, who were either compelled to stay back for their employers, the EIC, or had no motivation to return to England. Another incentive for the English officials of the EIC to stay back was the lure of additional money. The temptation was enough to brave the presence of killer diseases such as malaria, diarrhoea and typhoid, which the swampy settlement offered by default. A description of the fervent ongoing business in the early years of the settlement stands testimony to this immense money-making.

> The three as yet unpromising settlements of Bombay, Madras and Calcutta were eventually to become power centers of British Rule in India. But the 17th century merchants were uninterested in empire building. They were too busy making money for the company and for themselves. During the busy season between September and November, the East Indiamen were able to sail, the factory courtyards were transformed into stock exchanges.[9]

They used 'country' (Indian) ships to ferry musk, spices, cotton and carpets across the Bay of Bengal or the Arabian Sea. Those

East India merchants who survived the diseases that killed most men within two years were able to amass large fortunes.[10]

A somewhat similar description is given by Dalrymple, who talks of the casualties and the new settlement's willful prosperity in the same breath. 'Within a year of the founding of the English settlement at Calcutta, there were 1000 living in the settlement but already Hamilton was able to count 460 names in the burial book: indeed, so many died there that it is "become a saying that they live like Englishmen and die like rotten sheep".'[11]

He offers a vivid description of how prosperous Bengal was:

> Only one thing kept the settlement going; Bengal was 'the finest and most fruitful country in the world', according to French traveller Francoise Bernier. With its myriad weavers—25000 in Dhaka alone—and unrivalled luxury textile production of silks and woven muslins of fabulous delicacy, it was by the end of the seventeenth century Europe's single most important supplier of goods in Asia and much the wealthiest region of the Mughal Empire, the place where fortunes could easily be made.[12]

Charnock wasn't surprised when Bengal emerged as the potential money-spinner but the others in the Company were. In fact, it was on the profit from the business of Bengal that the EIC's goals were materializing. The need to secure the earned monies by building a fortified station was most imperative now. However, Charnock's vision of the fortified station aka Fort William remained unfulfilled during his lifetime primarily because he 'was old and enfeebled, and his subordinates had got out of hand. Before his death, on the 10th of January, 1693, from protracted illness, Charnock had acquired the jaghirdar's pucka cutcherry'.[13] Though the land was acquired, the actual building of the Fort was still in the air, as was the Company's legal status.

Charnock tried though. 'Since 1690, when he landed at Sutanuty, a process was initiated which sometimes systematically but mostly haphazardly made a city out of the existing site.'[14] He died in less than three years after having chosen Sutanati. Once the fort came up, his choice proved infinitely wise in no time.

Wilson, too, like Ray, paints the information of Charnock's death in a realistic description.

The many hardships he had undergone during his long sojourn in India now seem to have taken effect upon Job Charnock. His health gave way, habits of indolence crept over him, his spirit failed him, his temper grew moody and savage, the reins of government slipped from his relaxing fingers. On the 10th January 1693, he died.[15]

Charnock's death impacted the management of the EIC in eastern India but could not interrupt the unfettered consolidation of trade. To implement this mission, the English finally began building the fort on the cutcherry (land for administrative building) land of the jagirdar Sabarna Roy Choudhury. The fort was named after William III, the King of England. Little did they know that in less than a hundred years, their dream fort would be crumbling apart. In fact, after Siraj ud-Daulah had sieged the new city and its only fortification in 1756, it came to be known as the 'Old' Fort William. 'It was located in Dihi Kalikata south of the Burra Bazar and extended from the middle of the Clive Street to northern side of the tank (Tank Square).'[16] The reference, of course, is in tandem with the present-day map of the city. What is important, however, is to understand the crucial positioning of Fort William, around which the town would gradually appear—almost like the emergence of characters in a Hayao Miyazaki film.

'The marvellous rapidity with which the United Company's Settlement at Calcutta prospered on the completion of Fort William excited the jealousy and cupidity of Prince Azim-us-Shan and Jaffar AH Khan and increased their exactions.'[17] Though jealousy and harassment were one of the reasons, they were the lesser evils. The more important logic behind the acquisition of the three villages—Sutanuti, Gobindopur and Dihi Kolikatah—was that the Company wasn't a bona fide tax collector, nor did it have any ownership of the land on which it had already built the fortification. It was in a cumbersome situation. The gains from being strategically located wouldn't be enough unless the three villages were acquired.

> The necessity for the acquisition of these villages arose from the fact that the English with their shops, shipping, servants, and dependents, their banians, brokers, and traders, who were most rapidly increasing in number, lay scattered, in spite of concentration of the factors and soldiers in and around Fort William, over the whole of this area in straggling houses and boats; and, without the rights and powers of a zamindar, it was becoming more and more difficult to deal with them in the best interests of the Company.[18]

The English understood the precarity of their situation. The bureaucratic cobweb and power dynamics among the local jagirdars, Roy Chowdhurys, the governor Shaista Khan and

Prince Azim-us-Shan in Delhi were complicated, but the Company officials were focused in their goal of advancing trade and garnering profits. So, they decided to go all out.

> In 1698, Prince Azim-us-Shan's farman elevated them, followed, as it was, by actual purchase of land from Ram Chand Ray, Manohar and others, to the position of a dependent talukdar but still liable to pay rent to the superior landlord, the jagirdar. The rent payable by them was fixed at Rs. 1,281-6-9 per annum. Thenceforward they settle tenants under them, grant them pattas, collect rent, allow houses to be built, register their sale and transfer, charge a registration fee and impose fines upon their tenants and servants.[19]

Yet, the deal was not secure. Small revenues started trickling in as tenure holder, but that wasn't enough. The Company decided to send a petition to the Emperor in 1717. 'In the petition of the English to the Emperor it was stated that the three villages—Govindapur, Sutanuti and Calcutta—had already been purchased by them from the zamindars, and approval to that transaction [given].'[20]

John Keay, in his *India Discovered*, has an interesting description of how the approval finally came through for the Company:

> The prayer of the company was granted, chiefly through the exertions of Surhaud, who again succeeded in obtaining for the Company a confirmation of their former privileges of trade, and also permission to purchase from the zamindars thirty-eight riparian villages on both banks of the Hooghly, extending to a distance of ten miles from

their factory. The object of the Company was to secure the full powers of a zamindar which were similar to those of a Magistrate-Collector of the present day in kind.[21]

What happened in the following years is complex, mind-boggling and, above all, a great journey of a small, irrelevant spot on the river Hooghly to what Robert Clive had passed his remark that Calcutta 'is one of the most wicked places in the Universe… Rapacious and Luxurious beyond conception'.[22]

AWAY FROM THE RIVER

With the petition granted, Calcutta's territorial bearings were established. The Company now had the right to shape up the metropolis to its need and advantage. 'This was an important moment for the Company embarking on a more ambitious territorial venture.'[23]

The new settlement, now addressed as Calcutta, stood on the Hooghly.

Once a defined territory was outlined, the need for Calcutta's urbanization was a priority for the EIC as well as the affluent Bengalis. The restructuring would reflect not only on the city's growth but also on the existing business patterns, and then further on to the lifestyle to which Calcutta would be drawn.

Calcutta was changing.

Sutanuty formed the northern part of the settlement extending from Baghbazaar in the north to the old mint in Burra Bazaar in the south. The area constituting the Burra Bazaar up to the Bow Bazaar area was designated as Bazaar Calcutta. This was followed by Dihi Kalikata in between the old mint and the Custom house (Old Fort William). It was the site of the European commercial quarter, around the Tank Square and St. John's Church adjoining the Burra Bazaar. This was Town Calcutta.[24]

With extended boundaries of the city charted out, those who wanted to trade looked out for hyperlocal spots that would allow them to run their business uninterrupted. Establishing markets would be the next task in hand.

Mukundaram Seth was the first in the Seth clan to move from Saptagram (colloquially called Satgaon) and settle in Gobindopur, setting up a market there. The Seths had an important role in how the city would evolve. To that, I find researcher Shrimoyee Basu's understanding tenable,

> They claimed to have established the cloth market at Sutanuty hat and bazaar. The particular space where the mart was set up was popularly called the Hatkhola Ghat or the Market Ghat, where skeins of thread and woven cloth were sold and was called so as the hat was held under an open sky probably even before the Setts and the Basaks arrived.[25]

While Hatkhola Bazaar is attributed to the Seths, narratives claim that there were other pre-existing markets too. These were hyperlocal bazaars that surfaced around the temples of Goddess Kali, or temporarily during festivities of Shyamray and Radha (Krishna and Radha), and finds mention in Ray's 'A Short History of Calcutta'.

> They mention that it was from the annual Holi festival of this very Sham Roy and his spouse, Radha, during which a vast quantity of red powder (Kumkum) used to be sold and scattered in and around their cutchery tank, in temporary bazars erected for the occasion that Laldighi,

Lalbazar, and Radhabazar derive their names, and further, that most of the inhabited spots of the time situated within the sacred area were named after the gods, such as Sivatala, Kalitala, Siddheswari-tala, Panchanantala, Sastitala.[26]

Ray further writes:

> The old zamindars of Calcutta further claim that it was the hât and bazar round their idols and their pucka zamindari cutcherry west of the tank that gave Calcutta its original importance and gave rise to the names of 'Hat-tala' (latterly corrupted into 'Hat-khola,' and Burrabazar (bura being a familiar name of Siva); that it was the dôles near the Kali's temple that attracted a large population and contributed to the reclamation and cultivation of marsh and jungle, and that their culverts, landing ghat and roads, with a shady avenue of trees on their sides formed the only adornment of rural Calcutta in its early days.[27]

Clearly, there were bazaars of different hues, but what is important to look into is how two elements worked in tandem—the urbanization of Calcutta as a city and the emergence of markets and market culture—like a slowly revealing metastory within the bigger novella.

As the Company officials started building the fort, the city, too, began expanding simultaneously. The urbanization was need-based, rather than being planned. 'Even at the best of times town planning was never one of Calcutta's more obvious virtues.'[28]

While the English population was concentrated in and around Fort William, the larger local population centred itself where the Bengali elites chose to be. Their settling in different pockets of the town would mean an emergent high life. Moving up, they also made settlements at Sutanuty, improved the place and turned it into their so-called 'suburban gardens', such as Sett Bagan, Jora Bagan, Kala Bagan, Goa Bagan and Ram Bagan.[29]

Interestingly, the growing town was not just about the English and local affluent families. Dalrymple mentions that: 'Since Charnock's death, Calcutta had quickly grown to become the jewel among the Company's overseas trading stations: it was by far [the] EIC's most important trading post in India and the major source of British textile imports.'[30]

He further adds:

The city's legal system, and availability of a framework of English commercial and formal commercial contracts, enforceable by the state, all contributed to making it increasingly the destination of choice for merchants and bankers from across Asia. As a result, by 1756, the city had a fabulously diverse and polyglot population: as well as Bengalis, and Hindu and Jain Marwari bankers, there were Portuguese, Armenians, Germans, Swedes and Dutch, some—judging by an early census—with sophisticated and sometimes bizarre skills: watch and clockmakers, painters, pastry, cooks, goldsmiths, undertakers and wig fabricators.[31]

This entourage of traders and essential, special-service providers were the human elements of the upcoming bazaar, in which everyday list of vendibles only got longer by the day. From tiger skin to ice, from cottage cheese to Belgian mirror—everything perceptible and imaginable were sold in these markets. The big question at this point is: how can a town that is not even 67 years old have so many bazaars and why were they expanding and flourishing? The answer is of course short and definitive: Calcutta was a safe haven for private entrepreneurship. 'Excess' was in the air, in the form of infinite cash flow. This directly had an effect on the boom that the markets saw.

In his typical brilliance of narration, Dalrymple goes on to give a hearty description of the town of 'excess' and consumption:

> Calcutta probably now contained around 200,000 people—though some wilder estimate put the figure at almost double that—of whom around a thousand were Europeans. The city's docks were as busy and bustling as its bazaars, and twice as many ships now visited it every year as docked at its Mughal rival, Hughli, a little mainstream. The Calcutta punch houses were always full of captain and their crews of boatswains, mates and pilots drinking away their sorrows before heading to Calcutta's notorious brothels.[32]

Taking it from there, the vivid imagery only foments the idea of how lifestyles must have been in this growing, prosperous city, beyond the dock area, in those European big houses that stood facing the river or the ones that belonged to the wealthy Bengalis located strategically near Burrabazaar, Pathuriaghata or Laldighi. What they wore, where they went for dinner, what their breakfast was like, who cooked for them, what their nautch events, picnics and hunting days were like—we can only imagine. There is so much to explore, but most importantly, it is about making sense of the immense changes that swept Bengali life and were there to stay for times to come.

The narrative of the culinary shift that was not in isolation can be attributed to the gradual yet somewhat drastic manner in which everything transformed as 'John Company' or the East India Company settled in Bengal. Jennifer Brennan writes in *Curries & Bugles*, 'They turned India from the wealthy exporter they had created into a consumer market of British goods.'[33] Now that could mean a hotchpotch of changes impacting the everyday life of Bengalis, to be specific upper-caste Hindu Bengalis, who mostly feted and, at other times, resisted these changes in their lifestyle.

Whether the imprints of the mix-up affected the language first or the food is the quintessential question of chicken or egg. However, it was for real that the spoken English language was also undergoing a change. The newly inducted words often seemed funny against the backdrop of what their etymology was, but in reality, they were signs hinting at the culinary reworks happening within Bengali homes.

Sir Henry Yule, the first editor of *Hobson-Jobson*, a glossary of colloquial words, notes the hybrid elements of the vocabulary that was reflective of the language of the times. For example, words such as 'curry', 'toddy', 'veranda', 'cheroot', 'loot', 'nabob', 'teapoy', 'sepoy', 'cowry' and many more. The way Sir Henry and his co-author Arthur Coke Burnell understood:

> Words of Indian origin have been insinuating themselves into English ever since the end of the reign of Elizabeth and the beginning of that of King James, when such terms as calico, chintz, and gingham had already effected a lodgment in English warehouses and shops, and were lying in wait for entrance into English literature.[34]

Yule and Burnell also traced back this fusion to Portuguese times, 'The conquests and long occupation of the Portuguese, who by the year 1540 had established themselves in all the chief ports of India and the East, have, as might have been expected, bequeathed a large number of expressions to the European nations who have followed, and in great part superseded them.'[35]

The selection of these words and their induction into *Hobson-Jobson* is an indicator of early European influences, particularly Portuguese, but not pertaining strictly around food and entertainment. Soon, the Portuguese vocabulary faded and English words found their way into the everyday language of the Bengali elite, with them being swiftly added to glossaries and print media of the time. Words such as 'curry' and 'chop' were here to stay, blending into the language of both locals and the British—the markers of a paradigm shift in culinary culture.

In one of the most interesting narratives on food in British India and contemporary England, Lizzie Collingham makes a mention of the English fascination for 'curry' and how nearly till the 1870s, it ruled both places: 'Curries came into favor as an excellent way of using up cold meat. The British in India sometimes curried cold meat, and this is the origin of the jalfrezi which appears in Anglo-Indian cookery books as cold meat fried with lots of onions and chillies.'[36]

More than any other presidencies under British Rule, it was Calcutta that became a site for these gastronomic convergences. By the middle of the eighteenth century, references of bazaars along with taverns, punch houses and dak bungalows offered fascinating impressions of the ongoing life. Areas such as Lal Bazaar were the hub of activities and had several well-known English mercantile agencies. William Carey in *The Good Old Days of Honorable John Company* quotes John Zephaniah Holwell, an eye surgeon, who also became a short-term governor, remark on Lall Bazaar as 'famous'.[37]

In another detailed description of Lal Bazaar that extended up to Bowbazaar, the pocket comes across as sophisticated, with a robust marketplace and scores of shops trading enthusiastically.

In *Old Time Taverns in India*, John Barleycorn Bahadur further adds to the description:

> Some years later (1768), it was said to be the best street in the Settlement but was full of petty shops and 'boutiques' where Bengalee traders made a precarious living. If length counts it was a straight road from the Custom House to what is now called Sealdah. The first part, from the Strand to what is now Wellington Street was called Loll Bazaar. Then there was a section known as Bow Bazaar, and the short, far end, was Boitakhana. The famous 'Bread and Cheese' bungalow was at the far end of Bow Bazar, and in 1776 at the height of its popularity.[38]

Influences trickled through different channels—routed through local markets, food imports from England, Spain, France and other parts of Europe, also via taverns and eateries that were venues for private galas, as well as through impromptu innovations by the cooks and khansamas. To that, there were cookbooks, and both British and Bengali women got actively involved in creating eclectic, scrumptious recipes published in these. Also, being able to cook a fine meal was indicative of a Bengali woman's efficiency in the kitchen, reflective of her skills as a homemaker and also gave her a mark of respectability. On the other hand, for the English women, it was about learning the tricks of survival in a province with hostile climate and an unfamiliar cuisine.

By the mid-nineteenth century, educated Bengali housewives were making attempts to imbibe their European counterparts by creating new wonders in their kitchens. In the following years, some even managed to get magazines on home management published for bhadramohilas (respectable women). These magazines carried recipes hitherto unknown and articles on how to run a perfect pantry and kitchen. For most Bengali women, including the ones who were married to Englishmen, cooking acted as an agency to gain their worth in their husband's perception and in social circles.

With the earliest printed Bengali cookbook *Pakrajeshwar* (roughly translated: the Emperor of Cooking), an instructive handbook, it was rational that the lives of literate Bengali women would start taking new turns. *Pakrajeshwar* was followed by *Byanjon Ratnakar* (Fashioning Gems out of Victuals) four years later.

Complicated-sounding recipes like fish dampokhta and chagmundo randhan (how to cook a goat head), were included in *Pakrajeshwar*, posing a challenge for Bengali women. The books surely set the mood for making new dishes and learning holistic culinary management.

Cooking as well as maintaining an ideal kitchen wasn't a simple task, as the cookbooks and magazines seemingly projected. Successful incumbents were taken seriously by their mothers-in-law and other womenfolk in the family, escalating their status at home and helping them strike a chord with many of these 'cold-meat husbands'! Indeed a subtle subplot, a game of making and being a 'good housewife' had begun, toeing the lines of English women.

By August 1863, *Bamabodhini Patrika*, one the most successful Bengali journals targeting a dedicated readership of educated Bengali women, was at the forefront. While the journal has been acknowledged as instrumental in sensitizing

Bengali women, helping them enter into the foray of male-dominated literature, *Bamabodhini Patrika* had also systematically created prescriptions for an 'ideal Bengali woman'. Through December to March, issues of the popular periodical published an episodic essay titled, 'Duty of a Bengali Woman', which included vivid details of how to create a wholesome pantry and a neat kitchen and manage them too.[39]

In its entirety, this is also a story of consumption, of supplier and the consumer and their mutual relationship, of identity and pride, projected images of Bengalis, how they wanted themselves to be seen and known, and lessons in public relations, leading finally to a narrative that has been high on intercultural exchanges, cross-pollination, oddball mixes and, of course, the big thing of colonialism.

From everyday extraordinariness served on the table to special celebrations, from routines of *burrah khana* (big dinner) to ballroom events and inauguration of hotels, from nautch parties to dak bungalow experiences, and hunting days to picnics, food was omnipresent in Calcutta's life through the eighteenth and nineteenth centuries, rolling well into present times. The following chapters will charter through this timeline, mull over the gastronomy of Calcutta, and try to answer the whys, whens and hows of Bengali cuisine acknowledging that it has undergone a fair amount of transformation.

2

'Turtles Dressed, Gentlemen Boarded'

In 1780, an intriguing announcement made by a hotel in Calcutta kept by Sir Elijah Impey's late steward and Sir T. Rumbold's late cook read: 'turtles dressed, gentlemen boarded and families supplied with pastry'.[1]

The advert, at first glance, reveals a swaggering high life of Calcutta, a picture of consumption, of plenteous abundance.

Dalrymple notes in *The Anarchy*:

> Calcutta itself had turned into a boomtown with a population of 400,000, more than double than that at the time of Plassey. Now known as the City of Palaces or the St Petersburg of the East to its British inhabitants and the Paradise of Nations, Zannat-Al-Bilad to the old Mughal aristocracy, the Company's bridgehead in Bengal was unquestionably the richest, largest and most elegant colonial city in the East.[2]

Another historian, Katie Hickman, draws a reference of Calcutta through English traveller, letter writer and merchant Eliza Fay's graphical letters. Fay landed in Calcutta in 1780 with her husband and instantly felt a connection with the city. She writes: 'The banks of the river are as one may say absolutely studded with elegant mansions, called here garden houses. These houses are surrounded by grooves and lawns, which descend to the water's edge, and present a constant succession of whatever delight the eye, or bespeak wealth and elegance in the owners.'[3]

The surrounding affluence comes across well in her observation, highlighting spectacular architecture showy enough for anyone willing to notice. The sight of the serene Hooghly 'together with [an] amazing variety of vessels continually passing on its surface, add to the beauty of the scene', writes Hickman.[4]

Beyond its apparent grand look, which caught the fancy of almost anyone who visited the city, Calcutta was thriving big time. Once urbanization began, many were willing to invest in the city, anticipating growth. The traditional landed gentry had moved to the city, forming the wealthy class. A.K. Roy, civil servant and city historian, while describing the earliest demographic pattern, mentions that:

> The western part of Calcutta formed the most populous, important and architecturally adorned quarters of the native town. It included Kumartoli, Hatkhola, Jorabagan and Barabazar, all stretching by the bank of the river. Here dwelt those powerful contractors who supplied goods for the Company's investment, and amassed great wealth. Here lived the chief banians who drove a thriving business and made large fortunes. The Setts of Murshidabad, with the wealth of princes, had a gadi (commercial seat) here. Many of the chief officers of the native Government, Rai Doorlub, Raja Manickchand and Futtehchand, had mansions in this part of the town. The Sikh merchant, Omichand, who is more famous for his big beard which has passed into a proverb, than for his wealth amongst native Indians, lived in his own house, north of the Laldighi, in the European quarter of the town.[5]

These and some more of the well-known elite Bengali families became the Company's partners in trade, with the Seths and the Basaks chosen as the Company's main broker. What all was being traded and who traded in what find a detailed description in Basu's *Bazaars in the Changing Urban Space of Early Colonial Calcutta*:

Calcutta on Your Plate

Apart from these big merchant houses, there were big firms who acted as auctioneers or commission agents during the late 18th century, like Messrs. King, Johnson and Pierce; Mouat and Faria; Stewart and Brown; Tullah & Co.; etc. The last firm became a big name in this business and carried on for almost fifty years. They sold and commissioned a wide range of articles from black bear and rabbit skin tippets to Persian attar or essence of roses to cider and other kinds of intoxicating drinks to guns to soda water to Madeira wine to even the Dharmatala Bazaar. The Europeans, it seems, also engaged themselves, apart from trading, of course, (in spices, clothes, liquor, wine, indigo, opium, salt petre, etc.), in manufacturing businesses dealing with carpentry, glass work, gun making, washing and mangling, distillery, jewellery, coach-making, etc. and catered essentially to the European population residing in the city.[6]

That surely is a vast selection of items and it naturally would need a multitude of bazaars. By the mid-eighteenth century, there were more than one important bazaar—'Soba (Sova Bazaar), Dobapara, Hautcola, Baugh (Bazaar), Charles (Shyam Bazaar), Sam New (New Shyam Bazaar), Bagan (Begum Bazaar), Ghasthola (Gasthola) and John Nagore (Jaun Nagar)'[7]—and they reflected a growing culture of consumption. Merchant establishments vied for a space in the most strategically located bazaars. Soon, bazaars and hotels became reasons for Bengalis to nurture an urge for aspirational living. The items sold in these markets were not meant for bulk use only but were associated to a delicate, luxuriant lifestyle.

An assorted, random list of items sold would comprise Belgian looking glasses, wines and spirits, cigars, jewellery, hair dryers, hats, tobacco, perfumes, cheese, thea aka tea, biscuits, sugar, oysters, ginger, coffee, sweet candies, and more. For the British and other Europeans, such products were indispensable in retaining their usual lifestyle, but for Bengalis, freshly christened into the world of unfamiliar luxury, it was a gateway to an aspirational life.

The East India Gazetteer of 1815 reported a long list that included food products and décor items, while *Hickey's Bengal Gazette* published advertisements for theatres, ballroom dancing, pricey exotic liquors and the newly opened confectionary shops. The imports were primarily of British origin as well as from the other colonies of the Dutch, British and Portuguese. These advertisements revealed more than meets the eye, indicating new purchases made by Bengalis. Carey writes: 'Messrs. Dring, Cleland and Co., on June 4th 1795, advertise "for sicca rupees and ready money," the [following] wines and liquors, and the prices at which they are offered will show what were the prevalent rates of the day on these articles.'[8] There were handpicked Madeira, French Claret, Cognac in gallons, Old Rum never sold in single but always in dozens. Words like 'superior quality' and 'handpicked' were added to boost the sales. Unimaginable as it may seem now, a gallon of Cognac would cost ₹3–8, while a dozen of raspberry and cherry brandy pints would be just ₹18 and were considered costly.

Cheese, a novelty, was introduced by the Portuguese and was also imported from England. There was no mozzarella or cheddar in the growing town but a fine variety called 'pine cheese' and, of course, Portuguese cottage cheese, which were named after the locations of their settlements like Dhakai paneer and Bandel cheese. The imported cheese would cost ₹3–8 in the measure of a pound, while the cottage cheese was the more prized one and considered far more exotic by the locals.

Exotic was in abundance then. 'Fine Hyson teas' were advertised 'in 1793 at 250 sicca rupees the chest, 125 the half, 64 the quarter, and nine rupees the seer'[9] and 'fresh oysters were advertised for sale at John Morris, Cossitohllah Street, at three rupees per dozen, July 1808'.[10]

Cigars were sought after by firangis and locals alike. 'Bhilsa, which is still famous for its preparation of the perfumed tobacco for smoking in the hooka, was, in 1793, very celebrated, and exported to Calcutta.'[11]

For the upper-class Bengalis, these were objects of desire and it was just a matter of time before they would soak themselves fully in a new social order. Soon, aspects of trivial daily life underwent changes for the baboos. When feverish, they would no longer rub a pinch of mustard oil on their chest, to which their olfactory cells were forever familiar, but chose instead 'real Manilla Segars or cheroots freshly arrived from Philippines at one rupee a bundle'.[12]

By the late-eighteenth century, well-off Bengali baboos played smartly in the game of money-making, leading an indulgent Anglophile life, as they worked up their ladders of fortunes. With more foreign-sounding products flooding the markets of Calcutta, upper-caste and upper-class Hindu Bengalis started turning in droves to shop, thus embracing a cosmopolitan life, which they hadn't really planned.

What they bought had expensive price tags and yet nothing remained unsold:

In 1821, Red sparkling champaigne (sic) sold at 45 Rs. a dozen; White do at 40; Still do at 35; Port wine at 25; Gin at 15; Hodgson's Pale Ale at 11: Brandy at 16; Cheese at

3 Rs. a lb. Hams at 2; Tart fruits at 3 Rs a bottle; Oysters pickled at 8 a bottle; Sauces at 2 Rs. a bottle; Spirits of wine at 4 Rs. a quart; Tea at Rs. 150 a chest; Sugar candy at 22 Rs. a tub.[13]

The rise of this social group was to forever change the non-European social life of the city. The EIC mostly helped them gain social status and wealth and they, in turn, facilitated the Company's profit-making enterprises. Additionally, locals would be rewarded with bonus, which a majority of the Bengali businessmen reinvested in their properties of their native villages or capitalized at the Calcutta Stock Exchange generating more wealth. All in all, it was a copious amount of money being made!

Money-making was viable as some of the baboos were educated, with access to the public world, including visits to government offices. To that, there were chances of social networking at invites—private dinners and nautch events. The cross-pollination had already begun, with Bengali men wanting to replicate the life of 'others', swooned over by their experiences in the company of British officials. Interpreted, this wasn't just about new culinary choices but in sum, a European way of life, a modernity equivalent to awakening.

The envisaged lifestyle wasn't easy to implement in the Hindu households on the grounds of religiosity, so the initial experiences were drawn from outside, through the hours spent at taverns, hotels and dak bungalows, while they undertook business travels across India and overseas leading to free interaction with the Europeans and with non-Bengalis.

Breaking away from what was insular to their social conditioning, these Bengali men learnt to dine differently and wanted to bring back home their wholesome experiences.

Some even secretly nurtured the fantasy of having a wife who would be able to cook or supervise similar menus that were served at hotels or at parties. The male desire was heady enough to veto forward a wholistic, reworked image of a Bengali woman on the lines of a Victorian 'completeness'. A leap was taken, with the new term 'bhadramohila' coined for educated Hindu and Brahmo (a reformist segment of Hinduism) women. Meredith Borwick informs, 'Bhadramahila was originally only one of these words used to describe the female members of bhadralok families, but it crystallized into the term for an ideal type, embodying a specific set of qualities and denoting a certain lifestyle.'[14] Borwick adds: 'The model was an attempt to synthesize the virtues of new and old, based on traditional Hindu womanly qualities mixed with modern features derived from the Victorian image of the "perfect lady".'[15]

The must-have attributes of this prototype woman would be a combination of a talented cook and a good housekeeper. Thus another Bengali term *sugrihini,* or the good housekeeper, was promptly conceived. 'The modern *sugrihini* was one who was skilled in the new ways of cooking as well as the old.'[16] The expectations were fairly high as this rather interesting statement from editor Girish Chandra Ghosh of *The Hindu Patriot* (founded in 1853) reflects,

> In the art of cooking they are remarkably advancing. It is no longer a simple soup or a dish of porridge which established the fame of a Hindu woman as a cook; she must master the mysteries of pillaos and know exactly the true colour of a kebab in order to pass for learned in the art; some even aspire to the glory of preparing fowl curry and cutlets in exact imitation of the Great Eastern Hotel.[17]

The above remark positions bhadramohila firmly in the kitchen and attributes an astute adaptability to cook the food of 'others'. Interestingly, what menfolk consumed when outdoors was prepared solely by male cooks of different ethnicity and religion. Soon, they wished for the same food to be replicated at home, including menus of hotels like the Great Eastern but by the women of the house. This was to be executed sooner or later as 'the home then had to substitute for the world outside'.[18] In the next chapter, I will discuss how it became doable; how women became that 'dream cook' at the turn of the century, dishing out the most tantalizing food. However, let us first take a peek into the outdoor life that triggered these definitive changes in the tastes of the elite, upper-class and educated middle-class Bengali men.

SOME BUSINESS, SOME LEISURE: THE OUTDOOR WORLD

Collingham in *Curry: A Tale of Cooks and Conquerors* writes:

> The British were conscious of the fact that although they had replaced Mughals as the ruling elite, in the eyes of the Indian subject they were still low-class traders. They therefore concentrated on projecting an image of themselves as an impressive ruling class. The Reverend James Cordiner who visited India in the 1820s noted that 'all classes of society here live sumptuously and many individuals expend from 2-10,000 pounds each annually, in maintaining their household'.[19]

Collingham holds this as her primary argument to understand the flashy English life in India. Having agreed on her argument, I would add that as much as there was an inclination to prove themselves an elite ruling class, it was also the humongous profit made out of trading that made their lavish lifestyle work.

Cheap, available hired labour was catalytic to this lifestyle. For every household activity one could imagine, including kitchen and pantry jobs, the English assigned a worker. Like an *aubdar*'s (water cooler) sole job was to keep drinking water always chilled. He was also the in-charge of precious stocked up ice, which came all the way from America.

In an orientation manual on Indian living meant for new army recruits, written by Thomas Williamson in 1810, he describes backstories from a dinner at an army mess in Calcutta. This was much before Reverend Cordiner's commentary. He informs, 'The *aub-dar* would generally arrive at the house well before the party began, to ensure that the water, champagne, Madeira, claret or pale ale were all well chilled.'[20]

This foppish lifestyle was by no means a one-off thing or a standard practice for army recruits alone. It was nearly the same for all who claimed to be living 'modestly'. James Augustus Hickey was one from the latter lot! 'Hickey was not a wealthy man by Calcutta standards, employed sixty three, including eight whose only duty was to wait at the table, three to cut the grass in the garden, four grooms and one coachman, two bakers, two cooks, a hairdresser and nine valets.'[21] Though not an EIC official, Hickey was differently influential. He was the founding editor of the *Bengal Gazette*, the first English weekly newspaper of Bengal, which never minced words.

Abundance of a wicked kind swept the urban society of Calcutta in the late eighteenth century. And to retain it, what would be best than to hugely reinvest in trade and some in personal lifestyle aka on the dining table, where the pride and the ego of the host lay.

Collingham writes,

> In Calcutta, the host could be expected to possess sufficient china and silverware to set the table out. At the dinner, the servants, 'delicately dressed all in white muslins and white or figured turbans and large gold earrings' would stand behind the chairs of their masters attending their needs. The *khansama* (butler) would change the plates and hand round the dishes; another more menial servant might employ a small *chowrie* (fan) of peacock's feather to beat away the flies.[22]

It is this existence of opulence that the wealthy Bengali men or baboos wished for themselves and so did their educated subordinates—the middle-class bhadraloks. Dalrymple observes: 'Nor was it British who did well out of this new boom or who lived extravagantly: Bengali merchant and money-lending dynasties also flourished. The Mullick family, for example, had rambling baroque palaces strewn around the city and used to travel around Calcutta in an ornate carriage drawn by two zebras.'[23]

In the beginning of this culturally appropriated life, 'access' was critical—to be seen, to be invited into the couture. For Omichund, the Seths, the Basaks, the Mullicks, Ramdulal Dey, Govindaram Mitra, Ramdulal Sarkar, and their likes, Bengal's very own millionaires, that was not too far-fetched. In no time, these Bengali heavyweights were a part of the gated community (read white town) and made themselves conspicuously present at important social gatherings. A.K. Ray makes a detailed note on the city history while working on the 1901 Census, 'It is remarkable that Omichand and the Setts, who were brokers to the Company, were the only native Indians whose names appear in the plan of the English quarter of the town.'[24] Ray even gives a precise location of these exclusive houses in pre-1757 Calcutta, 'Omichand, the Sikh millionaire, had his house on the north of the tank, while Rasbihari Sett and Ramkissen Sett had theirs on the west of the burying ground.'[25] Owning a residential mansion was not enough; it was a fall-off if you didn't have a 'garden house', one meant for private life.

Arguably, Omichand was favoured, for the British kept the chief salt broker, the Company's prime business agent and banker in good humour by returning his favours for supporting the EIC in ousting Siraj ud-Daulah. The broker-financier led a royal life. He had more than one lavish palaces strewn across Calcutta and Bengal and had made a strong clout as a private financier. The British were in awe of his money power. The rest of the Bengali gentry was clever enough to woo the British with what they enjoyed most, other than profit-making—being entertained.

Most of them owned garden houses and needed no excuses to throw extravagant gallas. Such parties meant free-flowing spirit and delicious food cooked by fine rakabdars and served by khansamas. A typical party menu could consist of fish in batter, shepherd pie, English roast, kebabs, plum cakes and red wines specially delivered from various wholesalers who, in turn, acquired them from France, Spain and Italy.

Ice was an absolute must in such parties—perhaps more precious than the gold and pearls worn by the female guests. The food served was pretty similar to what the British had as their 'crowning meal of the day'—the burrah khana (i.e. dinner that was often served by four o'clock in the afternoon). 'The burra-khana was the focus of Anglo-Indian social life. It was on their dinner table that the British in India most extravagantly displayed their wealth and status. Amazed commentators remarked that there was always so much food "that no part of the table-cloth remains uncovered".'[26]

Collingham also describes some of the actual dishes that often showed up on the table.

> Turkies that you could not see over—the round of Beef, boiled roast Beef, stewed Beef, loin of Veal for a side dish and roast big capons as large as Hen Turkies. Large bowls of curry and rice, were placed along in between the turkeys and beef. This was just the first course.[27]

A dinner line-up of Mrs Fay, who apparently lived cheap, read, 'I will give you our bill of fare. A soup, a roast fowl, curry and rice, a mutton pie, a fore-quarter of lamb, a rice pudding, tarts, very good cheese, fresh churned butter, fine bread, excellent Madeira (that is expensive but eatables are very cheap).'[28]

Whether cheap or lavish, all dinners were followed up with mandatory drinks and hookah sessions. Interestingly, reams have been written on English lifestyle, but nothing like the wry humour of Dennis Kincaid in his *British Social Life in India*,

> Wine was, during dinner, generally diluted with water. When dessert had been served and a few loyal health drunk, the ladies withdrew and the gentleman sat down to the serious business of three bottles of claret each. It would have seemed oddly unsocial for a gentleman to drink less when as Mrs. Fay wrote 'every lady (even your humble servant) drinks at least a bottle'.[29]

This for the affluent Bengalis would be accessible only outside the domain of their homes. Thus, the sure-shot way to secure pleasures, as Europeans did, was to visit hotels, taverns and dak bungalows, and get into an immersive outdoor life at large. When this was adapted, at 'home' level, it was the *ginni* (the lady of the home) who was the visible actor in transforming Bengali houses into semi-Victorian set-ups, in particular the kitchen and the pantry. Her story merits a detailed discussion, which I will touch upon in the next chapter. For now, I must refer to Utsa Ray, who studies History of the Middle-Class, Taste and Consumption, and South Asia (History), in explaining how proactive Bengalis were in embracing the 'modern'.

> In this making of the 'Bengali' cuisine, colonized subjects were themselves the actors. The construction of a Bengali cuisine through the daily rituals and practices surrounding food in colonial India reveals a process of indigenizing modernity, whereby the colonial was critiqued at the same time as a colonially-produced middle class succumbed to the pleasures of the modern.[30]

The growing modernity was also a part of self-fashioning, an imaging that Bengali men desired in order to make themselves socially relevant to the British. Food was the easiest map to follow; however, this also meant consumption of 'forbidden foods' like meat and alcohol. Public life therefore needed an upscaling. The desi millions which they had invested in the business of textiles, indigo, saltpetre, etc. were returning huge profits. The local gentry left no stone unturned in creating the replica of a white man's lifestyle.

Kitchenscapes were altered by lavish parties as well as by the dak bungalow and tavern experiences. 'Wealthy Indians responded by installing in their houses English kitchens, staffed by Muslim cooks. This meant that they could provide for British guests without compromising their own vegetarian kitchens.'[31] They competed against each other to hire the best rakabdars, bawarchis and khansamas for special parties, who would be then entrusted with various meat and poultry dishes, both Mughal and European. From laying out a tablecloth to cooling a bottle to checking on the temperature of the ice, every little detail was taken care of in these parties. There were cooks, a cook's mate and a *masalchi* (spice grinder and dishwasher). There was a khansama and a second butler to wait at the table, assisted by an aubdar and a *khidmatdar*. These were Victorian standards of 'perfection' which became the norm. 'With food and drinks set, the extension of luxury and plentitude reflected in the nautch parties, the contemporary chroniclers have sometime added the escalated sensuality and romance in it like Mrs. Sophie Belnos who was completely smitten by the world of these nautch parties and made attempts to write and sketch what she experienced.'[32]

In *Nautch Girls of the Raj,* Pran Nevile narrates how smitten Mr Belnos actually was:

> In her vivid description of a dance party, held in Calcutta during the Puja festival, she observed: On entering the magnificent saloon, the eye is dazzled by a blaze of lights from splendid lustres, triple wall shades, chandle (sic) brass, etc., superb pier glasses, pictures, sofas, glasses, chairs, Turkey carpets, etc., adorn the splendid hall; these combined with the sounds of different kinds of music, both European and Indian, played all at the same time in different apartments; the noise of the native tom toms

from another part of the house; the hum of human voice, the glittering dresses of the dancing girls, their slow and graceful movement; the rich dresses of the Rajah and his opulent Indian guests; the gay circle of European ladies and gentlemen, and the delicious scent of attar of roses and sandal which perfumes the saloon, strikes the stranger with amazement.[33]

Such was the fame of these dizzyingly opulent nautch that even London's *Asiatic* journal, far from sight of happening, featured them. In October 1832, they published a pre-event news feature about Babu Muttelall Mullick's nautch adorned by the legendary courtesan Begum Jahn and Hingum.

The advertisement-cum-news report preceded the event,

The Hindoo holidays of Durga Puja have begun. Many of the rich Hindoos vying with one another in expenses and profusion endeavour in the richness of their festival to get a name amongst men. The principle days of entertainment are the 20th, 21st and 22nd; on which Nickee will warble her lovely ditties at the hospitable mansion of Rajah Kishun Chand Roy...nor will the hall of Neelmoni Mullick resound less delightfully with affecting strains of Ushoorun who for compass of voice and variety of note excels all the damsels of Hindoostan.[34]

Top-notch courtesans who were hired from Agra, Delhi and Lucknow commanded a hefty price. There were elaborate arrangements made—from invites to impeccable menus, which could even go up to a seven-course meal spread. A well-designed menu was to be carefully planned and the strategization was somewhat as followed in England. A description of a set menu by sought-after chef Oscar of the Waldorf is an eye-opener, a work of accuracy. I am including here the details of one of his multicourse menus. The menu accounts invitee's status and the season when the event took place. He writes,

> The menu should be strictly followed in every case. If the dinner is to include ladies, it should be of light, fancy dishes; but, on the contrary, if intended for gentlemen alone, it should be more substantial and at the same time shorter.
>
> The color of the various meats and sauces should be as different from each other as possible, from one course to another, offering all the foods in their respective seasons, and have the early products of the finest quality, and only use preserved articles when it is impossible to obtain others.
>
> Oysters, as a rule, are always served at the beginning of a dinner.[35]

The same was followed by the British here, with few mandatory local dishes added. Often that would be sweet-and-sour mango chutney and fried fish. These had won European hearts as did curries, kedgeree (khichri) and mulligatawny soup. 'Dinner at half past seven or eight consisted of soup, and entrée, roast fowls or ducks, occasionally mutton, and in cold weather once or twice beef, an entremets of game or a savoury, and sweets.'[36]

Observingly, those who wrote manuals for the English readership headed for a job posting in India often highlighted the futility of Eurocentric dinner menus. In one such manual in which the author disguises with the nom de plume 'Anglo Indian' emphasized on the availability of local ingredients and foremost the brilliance of the house steward or khansama, who could turn any dinner into a most delectable experience for the host as well as for the guest.

It is a mistaken idea that in India you should set before your guests as many English dishes as possible. The consequence is, you have tinned salmon, tinned peas, tinned ham, bottled fruits, and what are generally termed Belatee (English) stores given [to] you at every dinner party until you are wearied at the sight of them, and loathe all tinned things for the rest of your life. There is no reason why those Indian fruits, vegetables, fish, game […] which are in season, should not be used; only we all so much resemble a flock of sheep we must do as our leader does; and as the fashion is to set as many English things as possible on the table, English people follow it ad nauseam.[37]

Almost in a confessional tone, he/she further writes,

A dinner party is always an event of grave importance to your cook, his dignity is at stake, he feels that on him devolves a grave responsibility, and if your guests are those who hold an important position in the station, either military or civil 'big wigs,' he will rise to the occasion, and give you and your guests a far better dinner than many cooks would at home. How the good dinners are cooked, which one partakes of in India, is a marvel, and I am always filled with astonishment at the way a good khansaman will manage with, literally speaking, only a few pots and pans, for a set of dechsies such as he uses would fill an English cook with scorn.[38]

Quite a eulogy, but it was indeed the mastery of those who cooked that made their patrons flock around the most famed hotels, taverns and coffee houses of the city. Branding happened by word of mouth within the coterie of the Europeans and the locals. Often, it would be the proprietors who cooked themselves a particular delicacy for which the eateries became renowned. Some rose to fame for their ambiance, if not strictly for their food. There were Apollo, Harmonic, Tresham, Le Gallais, Esplanade Hotel, Chowringhee Hotel, The Spence's Hotel, The Grand Hotel, The Peliti's and The Coffee House, and all had their unique positioning. Harmonic, the earliest Euro-fashioned tavern of Calcutta, came up before any hotels and was a go-to for the bigwigs.

'In 1780 the Harmonic Tavern in Lall Bazar was the centre of social exaltation, something of a Bohemian Club, more than a tavern of the class that was general then, but nevertheless, a tavern. The building was the handsomest house in the "Settlement" where Society reigned.'[39] Mrs Fay stated in one of her letters that Mrs Hastings (the wife of Governor General Warren Hastings) was a regular patron of the Harmonic Tavern, holding a kind of court whenever there.

Interestingly, it was Charnock who had started the first tavern of the city with his partner Captain Hill, but it failed big time, letting the Harmonic bag the tag of the 'first tavern' of Calcutta nearly hundred years later. Hill, Charnock's business partner, was notoriously ill-famed as an indulgent man and Charnock is said to have not gained much from the tavern as an extra income. The EIC raised Charnock's pay from £20 to £40 per annum and later added a mere gratuity of £20. Thus, the benefits from the tavern was perhaps something

Charnock had hoped for, but it never happened. Nothing more is known about Charnock's tavern though.

Unlike the Harmonic Tavern, which was high on its ambiance, food was the sole reason for the popularity of Federico Peliti's restaurants in Calcutta and Simla. An Italian who served as the personal chef of Viceroy Lord Mayo, Peliti's destiny brought him to the city when he won a confectionary competition in Paris!

Peliti fell for the vibrancy of Calcutta and after Mayo's sudden assassination in Port Blair, he returned to the city to open a bakery at 41 Bentinck Street with his partner Thomas O'Neil. However, the partnership failed and Peliti moved out on his own to a larger premise in Chowringhee (downtown of even present-day Kolkata). He bought an imposing property at the heart of the city—10 and 11 Government Place East, adding a restaurant to his confectionary outlet. Soon, it was one of the best and the most favourite meeting hubs for those who wanted to be seen enjoying a delicate meal followed by Peliti's famed teacakes and Darjeeling tea.

For the connoisseur, Peliti came up with an exclusive vermouth (also spelt 'vermut'). In 1872, Peliti's vermut was produced for the Prince of Wales, Edward VII and it received gold medals at the international exhibitions in Turin, Paris and Calcutta. The secret of its success was its recipe: a mixture of well-blended Indian spices and Piedmontese flowers with bitter notes of absinthe combined with the sweetness of Muscat Passito. A flavour that combined tradition and exoticism; in other words, a flavour that was the mirror of its time; a sort of manifesto of a Belle Époque, whose wave of progress and wealth would subsequently be shattered by the harsh reality of world conflicts. Such had been the legend of his infused, fortified wine that it is still held as a treasure trove on the family's website—a much-guarded secret recipe.

Advertisements for these taverns and restaurants were sometimes outlandish, hidden with clever business ideas laced with humour. Towards the end of the eighteenth century, one advert of a tavern read somewhat like this:

> Ladies and Gentlemen may be furnished with Dinners, Suppers, or Cold Collation, on the shortest notice. Biscuits of all kinds, tarts and tartlets fresh every day. He also prepares the following articles for Sea, or to take Up-country, which he will warrant for six months:—viz. Potted Beef, Veal, Mutton, Ducks, Geese and Pigeons, Collard Beef, Mutton, Pork, and small Pigs, Fish Coreach, Mince Meat, Plumb Cakes, Jams and Marmalades of all kinds, preserved butter, eggs and milk, milk-punch, etc. etc.[40]

That is a prolific menu even by today's standards, along with cool offers for takeaway.

Early coffee houses served freshly brewed coffee and sandwiches to their politically aligned elite clientele, into which select bhadraloks, too, got entry. One Francis Le Gallais had one such coffee house which started in 1775, near Harmonic in Lal Bazaar. It was a hub of British lawyers and their Bengali affiliates. Richard Barwell, their major patron, a lifelong aide of Hastings and a member of the Supreme Council of Bengal, always wanted his coterie of British and local affluent acquaintances to gather at Le Gallais every fortnight post-trial sessions of the sensational case of Maharaja Nando Kumar. 'During the notable trial of Nahda Kumar, Le Gallais provided for the lawyers and those whom they should invite "eight dinners and nine suppers for 15 persons each" for "which he charged ₹629".'[41]

Le Gallais hosted lunch and suppers and even New Year parties. Here, coffee would cost half a crown or 1 rupee and would come with city newspapers like *The Calcutta Chronicle* and the *Calcutta Advertisers*. Restricted entry in most of these eateries or the inability of having 'new food' at home could not dampen the spirits of Bengalis. They continued to manoeuvre their situation by luring the Europeans to their private parties or by visiting these hotels and restaurants that were coming up fast and frequently by hook or by crook. 'These hotels formed a convenient locus for those who could easily gorge on to a chicken cutlet without being concerned of polluting their home. At the same time the pleasures of eating out can be realised in these new public eateries.'[42]

The taste that enticed the affluent and later the middle-class Bengalis on their food plate was reflective of the overall luxury they were willing to embrace. It was not that they were not used to abundance, but this was more than that. 'Taste was definitely associated with pleasure and luxury,'[43] but the interpretation of luxury was way different than before. 'Luxury no longer simply meant opulence or excess. Instead, luxury or pleasure was also [the] manifestation of enlightenment and bourgeoise (*sic*) modernity, of fashion and global commerce far removed from display of courtly splendour of earlier times.'[44]

They were approving of an openness equivalent to modernity, which also meant enlightenment. It is in this groove that the Bengali gentry situated themselves. The Europeans then became the 'other' and appropriating their lives was thought to be the perfect mash of newness and an acceptance of a cosmopolitan or non-Hindu way of life. A conscious self-fashioning, connected to new identity building was emerging at the turn of the nineteenth century. Tastes for this burgeoning identity reflected nearly in all aspects of their lives—from the design and decor of their garden houses and mansions to their dressing style and mode of transportation.

Food choices invariably were the most apparent signs of embracing modernity. Bengali men were now accustomed to new eatables bracketed as pleasures like chicken cutlets, tea, soda punch, biscuits, cakes, pastries, fowl curries, sandwiches, puddings, kebabs, pulao and soups, not in this order though. They were hooked to the idea of good food that was associated to this list of delectables.

Rajshekhar Basu, a Bengali author and humourist, describes in one of his short stories the obsession that grew around new food, a hybridity away from what Bengalis formerly knew as their own cuisine.

> Ratarati (Just in One Night), a short story written by Rajsekhar Basu (who wrote under [the] non de plum Parashuram), the famous Bengali satirist demonstrated this point. In Ratarati, Charan Ghosh, a middle-class gentleman, came to a hotel named Anglo-Mughlai Café located somewhere in Calcutta with his friend Mr. Chatterjee in order to find his son Bantul. Charan Ghosh was aghast by the smell of meat in the restaurant. However, the restaurant was full of young customers like Bantul who took delight in devouring items of food like French Malpoa (a Bengali sweet resembling pancake) made from chicken.[45]

A little over the top, as was humourist Basu's style, but French chicken malpoa, a fictitious dish, surely hints at the transformation of gastronomic choices of a section of Bengalis.

Bengalis, like their English counterparts, had started travelling frequently for a reason or two more than what was envisaged earlier. Sometimes, it was for official business and on other instances, it was a retreat to their native places on celebratory occasions like Durga Puja holidays. This meant travelling for days and nights, halting at dak bungalows and steamer stations.

Around 1847, a decade earlier to the First War of Independence, there were early references of dak bungalows: 'Every fifteen miles or so, along the roads most frequented there are bungalows, (cottages on a ground floor) where you may stop and breakfast, dine, and enjoy the luxury of a cold bath.'[46]

A similar description but with a precise indication of the expenses at a dak bungalow appears in William Delafield Arnold's novel *Oakfield: Or, Fellowship in the East* published a few years later, in 1853. Arnold, who compared the dak bungalows of India to the inns of England, wrote, 'Small houses erected every forty or fifty miles along the great roads, where travellers may obtain shelter for twenty-four hours by paying a fee of one rupee.'[47]

Hobson-Jobson, the Anglo–Indian dictionary, added details to the state of affairs at a dak bungalow in their entry of 'dawk bungalow' (variently spelt) as 'a rest house for a weary traveller with some basics of a bed and a table, a bathroom and a servant serving food [at] a very moderate cost'.[48]

None of these descriptions were exaggerated; dak bungalows definitely made the Englishmen cringe for it was a far cry from their luxurious life in Calcutta. On the contrary, it was the same dak bungalow and its food experience that appealed to the Bengali travellers in the mid-nineteenth century, for whom it was a novelty. The pleasures of a dak bungalow meal, an innovative platter, which was quickly pulled off by the khansamas, was much cherished. It was beyond their regular 'home-cooked' food, a fanciful deviation.

Situating dak bunglows in the English food historiography, Collingham has her own take on this. Interesting how the word 'notorious' comes into play:

> In the 1840s, a network of dak bungalows was built which provided the traveler with food and a place to rest. These soon became notorious for their cookery. The [dak] bungalow khansaman, knowing that he has no other condiment whatever to offer to the hungry traveller, will, when asked, unblushingly profess to provide every delicacy of the season; but when appears and uncovers his dishes, there is fowl, nothing but fowl of every age, size and degree of toughness.[49]

In another rather hilarious conversation between a traveller and a khansama who would often double up as the in-charge, it's not difficult to sense how frugal a pantry of a dak bungalow was.

> The traveller on arrival has to sign the visitors' book and is asked 'Does your Honour require a meal?' He expresses his ability to supply 'What Master pleases.' Considering all things, it is astonishing what can be put on the table from that time a chicken is running about loose, hungry and happy, to being served up as soup, grilled, curried and roasted, with a brown custard, to finish, by the time the traveller has bathed and dressed.[50]

Collingham extends her thoughts and even connects it with the birth of the curry, which became immensely popular during the earlier years of the EIC. She writes,

The ubiquitous chicken was often presented to the traveler in the form of 'country captain,' one of the best-known Anglo-Indian curries. There are many different versions of this dish but basically it was a curry of freshly killed chicken flavored with turmeric and chillies, both ingredients that kept well. Nobody knows how the curry acquired its name but some suggested it was invented by the captain of a 'country' (i.e. Indian) boat. It was certainly frequently served to the British when they were 'up-country' traveling by budgerow or dak.[51]

The British, most of the time, were weary of this quickly rustled up fowl curry, but nevertheless survived days of travels on it. To that the less racist, lesser colonial-minded acknowledged the hard-working, smart lot of khansamas who were never short of innovating impromptu dishes.

An infinite variation of poultry dishes could be generated from the quintessential dak bungalow fowl, which along with other preparations such as chicken jalfrezi, and also teatime custard and an occasional milk punch were easy to rustle up for the often-lone man on the job and quickly serve the fatigued traveller. And thus, till date, there isn't any standardized recipe of the dak bungalow chicken.

Pertinently, the skills of the bawarchis and khansamas (many of whom were trained at the Mughal provincial courts, like Awadh) had been greatly appreciated too; the main reason for that being their vast knowledge of Indian spices and keen adaptability in accepting British food. They can be credited as key players in shaping Anglo-Indian cuisine and a sizeable portion of Bengali food. To their praise, Emma Roberts, the English traveller and poet, was vocal,

They would produce fish of every kind: fresh, dried, pickled or preserved, or hermetically sealed in a tin; delicate fricassées, rissoles, croquettes, omelettes and curries of all descriptions; cold meats and games of all sorts, jellies and jams from London and Lucknow, fruits and sweetmeats; with cakes in endless variety, splendidly set out in china, cut glass and silver.[52]

The English budgerow traveller was in a slightly more comfortable situation than his counterparts lodged in dak bungalows and yet food was still on the go, cooked in a jiffy with rudimentary ingredients.

An understanding of how stratified travellers' privileges were, almost like present-day perks, emerges in the following quote by Collingham.

Travellers who went by budgerow or dak caused less devastation. They would buy from the villagers 'boiled and smoked milk in earthen pots, [and] very small eggs of doubtful age', but otherwise budgerow travellers were served by a cook-boat which would draw alongside at mealtimes to serve passengers hot rolls for breakfast and meat curries in evenings.[53]

A separate cook boat was an exclusive privilege meant for British travellers. However, both firangs and desis had to have meals made by the *khalasi* or the boatman's aide.

Returning home for holidays to the eastern part of Bengal meant travelling by a night train from Sealdah in Calcutta and getting dropped at the Goalondo railway station (in present-day Bangladesh). An illustrated railway handbook published in 1913 explains the geographical location of the quintessential halt station Goalondo. 'It is situated at the junction of the Padma, or Ganges, and the Brahmaputra, and daily services of steamers connect it with the railway systems at Narayanganj and Chandpur, and with the steamer services to Madaripur, Barisal, Sylhet, and Cachar.'[54]

The same handbook notes Goalondo as an immensely strategic transit terminal as passengers undertook further travels:

> To visit Bengal without travelling on the great rivers which intersect that province would be almost as bad as going to Agra without seeing the Taj Mahal, and one may see something of the rivers and appreciate their importance as highways of commerce without making the long journey to Dibrugarh. For example, if one goes from Calcutta to Dacca, the rail journey is broken at Goalundo and from there to Narayanganj is continued by steamer. The night mail from Calcutta deposits one at Goalundo in the early hours of the morning, and there is little time for the tourist in a hurry to see much of this village and to appreciate its importance as a trade centre before he leaves on the steamer for Narayanganj.[55]

While the handbook was simply intended to promote the ease of commuting facilitated by the Eastern Bengal Railway after its launch in 1871, the Goalondo railway and steamer station became famous by word of mouth.

The passengers who travelled on the night train, exhausted from the tedious itinerary, would be eager to reach home. There was no concept of packed meals and therefore what was readily available on board was the only option: a light spicy, thin gravy preparation of country (desi) chicken with some basic spices cooked instantly. Thus appeared a close cousin of the dak bungalow fowl curry, which came to be called the steamer chicken curry.

Goalondo's terminal station was active till 1964 but ceased to function once the Indo-Pak War of 1965 began. Meanwhile, the steamer fowl curry attained its generic name for all steamer station chicken-based dishes across many ferries of West Bengal and the then East Pakistan. The dish Goalondo steamer fowl curry became the quintessential 'fiery, thin red curry with oil floating on top' and attained a better remembrance through the travel writings of one of Bengal's most celebrated authors, journalists and travel enthusiasts, Syed Mujtaba Ali. Originally from Sylhet in Bangladesh, Ali's writings take a deep note of the skills of the fowl curry made by unlettered boatman's assistant. He was a keen observer and high on life, and his musings invariably rolled back to food.

In 2010, his nephew and well-known diplomat Syed Muazzem Ali, on a Facebook page dedicated to Syed Mujtaba Ali, fondly mentions his uncle's love for food as well as his own childhood memories of the Goalondo Steamer Station.

My father was a member of Assam Civil Service and after partition, he opted for East Bengal. Our first exposure to East Bengal was when he was posted to Pabna in 1949. The mighty Padma-Meghna rivers overwhelmed us but the bigger surprise was those huge paddle boat 'Steamers' named Ostrich, Emu, Kiwi, Gazi etc. On board those steamers, delicious food items such as smoked Hilsa, chicken curry and cutlets, mutton chap etc were served. Uncle Mujtaba mentioned about Goalando ghat curry a number of times.[56]

Calcutta on Your Plate

Clearly, the boatman's culinary skill was highly rated and has influenced halt-station food within the larger Bengali cuisine, albeit tad romanticized.

Romance continued till the early part of the last century as discerning Bengalis went on detox vacations (*hawa badal* in Bangla) on the lines of summer holidays of the British. They parked themselves in these dak bungalows, some of which were still up and running. When they returned from their short sojourns, they would attempt to recreate the menu in their own kitchens or look out for an opportunity to eat out in hotels, cafés and small eateries, reliving the dak bungalow pleasures. The present-day resurrection of the dak bungalow chicken curry, Goalondo chicken and hilsa curry are intensely laced with nostalgia quotient from the colonial era, particularly from pre-Partition days.

Three decades after India's independence, in 1970, filmmaker Satyajit Ray made *Aranyer Din Ratri* (Days and Nights in the Forest). It is a story of four friends on a brief detox holiday, obsessed with lodging themselves in a forest dak bungalow, despite the lack of any official booking. Soon, their holiday would get complicated by a chance meet with two urban women and an indigenous Santhal woman. Throughout the movie, Ray shows food like chicken curry, toast, boiled eggs, which are the essentials of an English breakfast, as metaphors, depicting their dependence on Calcutta's food habit and the inability to cut off from the routine of city life, as well as their romanticization of dak bungalow lives erstwhile lived by the Europeans.

The reaction of Shekhar, one of the four men, a kind of jester for the group of friends, is remarkable as they are supplied with a can of boiled eggs by their recently made female friends in the climax sequence. The brief scene reemphasizes robust fascination for colonial food that Bengalis en masse had developed by the 1970s, the groundwork of which lay a century ago, as the first batch of hotels came into existence.

In few years, the enterprising Bengali merchants realized the potential of extending their love for food into a business. By the 1940s, several eating places cropped up in Calcutta. These were tiny eateries such as Basanta Cabin, which served toast and boiled egg, all ran by Bengalis. Two other small hotels called Café-de-Monico and Bengali Restaurant were established around 1936. Usually packed, these hotels served the 'new' food that Bengalis were drawn to like toasts, tea, omelette, boiled eggs, biscuits, fowl cutlets and cakes.

One such eatery was Chachar Hotel. The story has it that it was the founder Gosaidas Patra of 'Chachar Hotel' (the name originating from the erstwhile owner of a tea stall, an elderly Muslim man, fondly addressed as Chacha) who came up with the recipe of fowl cutlet, categorically promoting a snack free of onion, ginger and garlic. The fowl cutlet of Chachar Hotel became hugely popular amongst the customers. By the 1940s, Chachar Hotel had a signboard and had started adding on more dishes like mutton seekh kebab, which was made of beef since its inception way back in 1875. Patra changed the main ingredient to goat meat.

By now, the Bengali affluent and middle class both had loosened up a bit in terms of their eating restrictions and had started relishing the exotic food including dishes made of mutton, or onion and garlic, which was no longer a big taboo. The shift was somewhat possible due to the availability of ingredients—raw, cooked and tinned—many of which were directly imported from their European origin. 'New pleasures had a much broader social spread even if to a limited extent. Since many of these food stuff were produced on a large scale, their price was naturally low. As a result, new food like tea could be consumed by those at the lower rung of the social ladder.'[57] The quickest and most relatable would be the availability of bread, biscuits and arrowroot resulting in the making of more fowl cutlets and puddings, among others, at home. This, fortified with the advent of printing technology, resulted in the publishing of many cookbooks. Thus, the pleasures of new edibles were no longer limited to dining outside home. I will further go deep into how women contributed to this shift, influenced by these cookbooks, magazines and even school curriculum that promoted cooking and good housekeeping, in the following chapter.

THE METIABURJ SUBPLOT

'Everything was fantasy and illusion, a myth, the origin of which had all at once become effaced.'[58] The remark is by Abdul Halim Sharar, the official chronicler of Nawab Wajid Ali Shah's life who ruefully regrets the loss of Lucknow and everything that stemmed from the city unjustly in the hands of the British. What was lost reflected the finesse of a wholesome Awadhi life and living.

The loss was unacceptable and the last King wanted to recreate a mini Lucknow at Garden Reach, or Matiya Burj (differently spelt as Metiaburj), where he spent a little over 29 years of his banishment. From renovating his palatial house that resembled Metcalfe Hall, to having a huge entourage of wives, affiliates, rakabdars, khansamas, bawarchis, masalchis, palanquin bearers and zookeepers, it was prolific lavishness even in exile.

Abdul Halim Sharar, the official chronicler of the royalties, writes:

> From the time of the King's arrival in Calcutta, a second Lucknow had arisen in its neighbourhood. The real Lucknow had ended and was replaced by Matia Burj. The same bustle of activity, the same language, the same style of poetry, conversation and wit, the same learned and pious men, the same aristocrats, nobles and common people. No one thought he was in Bengal: there was the same kite flying, cock fighting, quail fighting, the same opium addicts reciting the same tale[s].[59]

The primary seed of refinement with which Awadhi culture is connected lies in the Mughal world; however, there is more to it. Awadh had adopted elements from the existing culture of the eastern Gangetic plains and made a unique identity for itself. Therefore, bracketing off Awadhi platter as merely an extension of Mughlai food would not be a well-thought assessment. Awadhi food is sublime, light and flavourful, the subtlety of which is rooted in the refined courtly culture of Awadh.

The pride of this fine culture was reflected best in Shuja-ud-Daula's rule in Faizabad, later passed on to others till it reached the regime of Wajid Ali Shah, the son of Amjad Ali Shah and his first wife Malika Kishwar, later known as Janab-i-Aliyyah, as he ascended to the throne in 1847. His brief rule in Lucknow, till by a quirk of fate he landed in Calcutta on a sultry day of May 1856, is described in the following paragraph. What happened thereafter in Metiaburj is but an extension of the Lucknowi life, which came with infinite tweaks in the political relationship between the King and the British government. Thus, knowing the ruler is a necessity leading up to a discussion about gastronomy which he brought from Lucknow to Calcutta.

Barring Bengali food that is known today, it is this Lucknowi culinary dubbed with a loose tag of 'Mughlai' in its form of biryanis, pulaos, rezalas, Mughlai parathas, kebabs and dopyazzas that had stuck back with the city. I can pretty much vouch for the potato-mandated yellow rice with a chunky mutton or chicken piece that Calcutta has lovingly embraced, intriguingly accepting it as its 'own'. Perhaps nothing is more Bengali than a Calcutta biryani, thus declaring the cosmopolitan in Bengali food.

We will come back to 'cosmopolitanism' in a later chapter, as for now, situating who the King was and what was his world view would be primary. All other cross-cultural influences were community-driven syncretic efforts. It is only in the case of the Mughlai/Awadhi food that it revolved mostly around a singular man, his personality, his army of culinary experts, laced by his personal choices, even when he had to adjust his purses. Nobody other than the last King of Awadh had influenced Bengali cuisine so head-on, with so much individuality.

Though the young royal was put into theological trainings, his natural instinct drew him to all things refined.

Sharar enumerates the King's pursuits:

He started to consort more frequently with beautiful and dissolute women and soon dancers and singers became the pillars of state and favourite of the realm. If the King had retained any scholarly or noble taste at all, it was for poetry. He himself wrote poems and had great esteem for poets.[60]

Sharar also judged the King's affinities and inclinations; however, in these descriptions, it is rather clear that the King was not an ambitious Muslim ruler who admonishing everything would set out on expanding territories. He was high on fine tastes and the seduction that life offered him through his wealth, his seal of royalty. Life in Lucknow was about 'gaiety' and this was to continue in Metiaburj too. 'This atmosphere prevailed in Lucknow and gaiety and merriment was the order of the day.'[61]

The same joy and passion was mirrored in Awadhi cuisine and a great deal of appreciation rested on the skills of its executors, especially the rakabdars and bawarchis. Awadhi rulers had picked up standard practices of cooking from Emperor Akbar's rule and took an interest in the good mix-up, innovating with ingredients even though less familiar. Perhaps the prominent example of being really innovative was their use of potato and pineapple in biryani and a dessert, respectively.

While the royals of Awadh have always reiterated that their food culture is unique and have fewer Mughal influences and more influences drawn from various cultures including the local east Gangetic elements like sattu (I will come back to it later), Collingham and others do track back traces to Mughal cuisine.

In the kitchens of Akbar's court, the chefs were expected to be able to serve up a meal of hundred dishes within an hour. The army of cooks came from Islamic world and northern India. Each brought with him his own regional techniques and recipes. The cooks learned from each other and out of this vibrant synthesis of culinary styles, emerged a core repertoire of dishes that constituted a new Mughlai cuisine.[62]

She adds:

> Besides synthesising the different cuisines by creating new dishes, Mughlai cuisine brought together the cookery of central Asia, Persia and Hindustan by combining different dishes from each of these traditions in one meal. In the pantry of the imperial kitchen, bakers made thin chapattis of Hindu provenance as well as the thick wheat breads, stuffed with honey, sugar and almonds, loved by the Persians. Persian cooks prepared sugar-coated almonds, pastries and quince jams, while Indian cooks made pickles and chutneys, sweet limes, curds, and green vegetables. These accompaniments of varied provenance were served with the main dishes to create a Mughlai meal.[63]

It was a fusion of many ingredients, several cooking techniques and experimentations, of believing in multitude and yet creating distinct flavours. The Awadhi cuisine is based on these principles as well and yet Mughlai food was distinct from the existing Indian food. Awadhi cuisine, too, is far from Mughal food. It is much less spicy, lighter and flavourful than its often compared counterpart, Delhi food.

In Awadh's royal environment, many kitchens functioned in tandem and cooks came from different parts of India as well as from other countries including the Middle East, Turkey, Iran and Iraq. Once appointed, the chef was much encouraged to carry out gastronomic experimentation seemingly individualistic. No one objected to these culinary trials in Lucknow and it was considered a practice in arts, much like music or dance.

To maintain this *shaukin's* (connoisseur) life, the Awadhi kings never restricted their budgets. Shuja-ud-Daula's regime was marked by glorious excellence in culinary and artistic culture. Nearly 70 years later, Wajid Ali Shah would adopt this legacy, engaging with everything that reflected a passion for the arts, including culinary.

Sharar pops an interesting anecdote:

Nawab Shuja-ud-Daula had his meals inside the Palace with his Bahu Begum. The maid servant brought the trays to the Begum, uncovered them in her presence and placed the food on the dastar khwan [tablecloth]. Each day food for the Nawab and the Begum, came from six separate kitchens. In this two thousand rupees a day were spent on food, so that, apart from the wages of cooks and other servants 60,000 rupees a month were spent on food and delicacies.[64]

All the six kitchens served delicious food for the Nawab, which involved much innovation. 'Thus from the time of Shuja-Ud-Daula, a very high standard of cooking was maintained. The very best cooks were enlisted, elaborate efforts were made in the preparation of foods and innovations were introduced. Expert cooks from Delhi and other places polished up their skills and invented new delicacies.'[65]

The precedence set a standard for Awadhi cuisine. The rulers believed in hiring the best cooks and their wages were non-negotiable. A cook's monthly salary could be ₹500–₹1,200 and upward and he would only be appointed for his skill in preparing a particular dish, which could be pulao, meat, paratha, kebabs, sweet bread rice pudding (gulathis), and so on.

Throughout his employment, he would be making only

that single dish and create innovations around it. Some of them would even set preconditions while being hired, something that was unheard of in that era. One of the cooks working for a relative of Shuja-ud-Daula, Nawab Salar Jung, once said that he would only cook for Salar Jung and no one else. Also, he would be cooking only pulao and no other dish. This would also mean employment of more people in running the royal kitchens. The structure of a Mughal and/or Awadhi kitchen would thus exist in strata.

Some mind-boggling details of employment, a breakdown of who did what at the royal kitchen, through Sharar's words, makes one wonder the scale of patronage and finesse related to culinary:

> Three classes of people were employed in preparing food. First there were the scullions who cleaned enormous pots and dishes and worked under the cook. Second was bavarchi, the cook, who prepared meals in large quantities. Third was rakabdars, the chef, who was the most expert and usually cooked in small pots for a few people only. He considered beneath his dignity to produce food in large quantities. Cooks too like to prepare in small quantities, but chefs never do otherwise because in addition to cooking they are occupied with the presentation and serving of food. They adorn the dishes with dried fruits cut into shapes of flowers, edible silver foils and other embellishments. They prepared light, delicious conserves and pickles and exhibit their skill in the gastronomic art in subtle ways.[66]

Even in his exile, Wajid Ali Shah's kitchen had more than 300 working staff, who continued on Awadh's legacy of innovation—the ultimate example of which was the inclusion of potato in their biryani, which later came to be known famously as Calcutta biryani. The inclusion of potato was more of an experimentation, which reflected the Nawab's ability to accept new-world ingredients—non-Islamic and completely cut off from his familiar food culture. He was quirky and unconventional. His experiments were artistic, driven by aesthetics and pleasure, be it playing the role of Kanhaiya (God Krishna) in Raslila theatricals or playing a banter on another noble called Mirza Asman Qaddar, a prince of Delhi, who was served murraba (a fruit conserve), which the nobleman realized was not a bowl of korma (quorma) but rather a camouflage! The Nawab was thrilled at his prankster self, while the guest was left feeling embarrassed at being outsmarted.

Biryani in its birth has been a synthesis of Hindustani spices and delicate Persian pulao—a fusion that originated in Mughal kitchens. Ironically, today's Calcutta has an unflinched loyalty to the biryani that originated in Lucknow; one of those mysterious gastro stories believed to be straight out of Wajid Ali Shah's kitchen.

Collingham writes:

Here, the delicately flavored Persian pilau met the pungent and spicy rice dishes of Hindustan to create the classic Mughlai dish, biryani. One of the most distinctive Persian culinary techniques was to marinate meat in curds (yogurt). For biryani onions, garlic, almonds, and spices were added to the curds, to make a thick paste that coated the meat. Once it had marinated, the meat was briefly fried, before being transferred to a pot. Then, following the cooking technique for pilau, partially cooked rice was heaped over the meat. Saffron soaked in milk was poured over the rice to give it colour and aroma, and the whole dish was covered tightly and cooked slowly, with hot coals on the lid and around the bottom of the pot, just as with pilau. The resultant biryani was a much spicier Indian version of the Persian pilau. Nowadays, it is a favorite dish in the subcontinent at all wedding celebrations.[67]

While the cooking technique remained essentially the same, somewhere along the way, every erstwhile Muslim province in India, like Rampur, Hyderabad, Moradabad and Bhopal, which boast some of the finest biryanis, added some unique ingredients to it.

Potato was a new introduction in the market, first by the Portuguese in the sixteenth century and later promoted by the British. The King may have agreed to add a piece of potato to his home-made biryani on the insistence of his rakabdars. For whatever reasons, potato got included in Calcutta biryani. I would credit the cook for his smart idea and the Nawab's approval of it post tasting.

The larger picture was built by the availability of hitherto unknown vegetables and fruits, quite aggressively promoted by the British.

As a historian on the 'History of the Middle-Class, Taste and Consumption', Utsa Ray's seminal understanding on this stands as below.

There was no aspect of food right from farming that didn't have a larger element of British colonial interest in it. Many of the new food crops introduced in India were a direct result of the 'Columbian exchange' and some of them came from Europe itself. These crops were chiefly introduced by the Portuguese traders in the 17th century. They brought in a number of crops with them, amongst which the most extraordinary was the introduction of potato. Tomato, okra and the ubiquitous chili pepper also came around this time. Amongst the fruits from the new world, most notable example is that of the pineapple. Grown in the beginning in the Portuguese possessions on the western coast, by the end of the 16th century, it became common enough in areas in the eastern parts of India like in Bengal. Although introduced by the 16th century, these vegetables never became a common item of diet until the 19th century when the British colonial state took the initiative to spread them on a much larger scale. The introduction of exotic vegetables by the colonial state had two purposes. One was to bring 'new' (modern) food to the subject population as a symbol of progress. The other was to recreate a sense of belonging for the colonizer in the colony.[68]

The British had a hunch that it would take long for these new fruits and vegetables to become popular. It was therefore a strategy to route it through a King who had some fan following and was well known for his quirks. Potato was one of the early vegetables of the newer lot, which over time turned into an addictive, indispensable ingredient in Bengali cooking, cutting across class, caste and even religion. It finally became a must in the quintessential Calcutta biryani, likely after Independence, when Bengal was still recovering from 1943's famine and the price of rice grains was exorbitant. Today, the most loved mutton or chicken curry of Kolkata is unimaginable without chunky pieces of potatoes thrown in.

Calcutta on Your Plate

Unlike the present day, mutton dishes weren't acceptable then, and consuming beef and pork was considered blasphemous. It was nothing short of serendipity that quorma was to become one of the oft cooked mutton recipes of Calcutta homes and Mughlai restaurants alike. I will come back to Lucknowi quorma soon. Meanwhile an interesting remark, reflecting Bengali resistance to new food or the food of 'others':

> One Bijayan Chandra Ghosh associated with railways observes, 'Many of us have started consuming indigestible English food Pulao (type of rice prepared with whole spices and clarified butter), Mutton curry, korma (generally a mutton or chicken dish made with yogurt, kebab and chop (a distortion of English lamb chop, cutlets and omelettes since Muslim rule. Technically speaking, most of the food items that he listed as English food can hardly be described such. However 'new' when associated with the 'other' became the object of suspicion'.[69]

Now the suspicion was directed not only to the fear of being jatibhrashta (outcasted) for consuming meat but also going off boundaries of home-cooked food which was believed to be 'pure food'. Either way it was about the process of 'otherization' and/or breaking the taboo.

Who can help break a taboo but artists, musicians, dancers, and their likes already labelled as 'fallen'. Most of them were fearless, and social ostracization was not a bother specially for the ones living in Metiaburj. It was a hub of mavericks, where many from the rest of Calcutta had no access to unless you were a well-known shaukin. Sharar writes:

They say that when the King first came to live in Matiya Burj he displayed such sagacity and his outlook on life became serious. On seeing this his entourage collected many musical instruments. Immediately the King was reminded of his old fancies and love for song and dance and as a result troupe of artist started to congregate at his court. The best singers in India were enlisted into the King's service and there was a larger concourse of musicians in Matiya Burj than could be found anywhere else in India.[70]

Observers believe that these nonconformists of Metiaburj later acted as catalysts in helping their specialties like biryani, rezala and kebabs to cross over to the rest of the city aided by the erstwhile Nawab's kitchen staff.

Apart from the present-day familiar rice dishes like Lucknow dum biryani and moti pulao, celebratory feasts worth talking about had more than 70 varieties of pulaos, all known for their *nazakat* (finesse and subtlety). Some of them even had poetic names, such as gulzar (the garden), nur (the light), koku (the cuckoo) and chameli (the jasmine). 'Oudh was famous for the "whiteness, delicacy, fragrance, wholesomeness" of its rice. It is unsurprising that the dish Lucknavis prided themselves on was pilau. In Delhi, biryani (the much spicier Mughal version of a pilau) was the most admired dish.'[71] 'To the uninitiated palate, both are much the same, but because of the amount of spices in biryani, there is always a strong taste of curried rice, whereas pulau can be prepared with such care that this can never happen. It is true that a good biryani is better than an indifferent pulau, for the pulau may be tasteless and this is never the case of biryani. But in the view of gourmets, a biryani is a clumsy and ill-conceived meal in comparison with a really good pulau and for that reason the latter was more popular in Lucknow.'[72]

The ultimate exhibition of white, delicate and fragrant wholesomeness was perhaps best exhibited in moti pulao, a pulao still loved. It is widely believed that moti pulao came into existence during the reign of Asaf-ud-Daula, the food-loving Nawab, conceived by one of his gourmet chefs called Haji Mohammad Fikir-e-Alam Saheb. Sharar describes,

> Moti, the pearl, pulau was made to look as if the rice contained pearls. The method of making these pearls was to take about two hundred grains in weight of silver foil and twenty grains of gold foil and beat them into a yolk of egg; this mixture was then stuffed into the gullet of a chicken and tied around with a fine thread. Well formed, shining pearls appeared which was cooked with the meat of the pulau.[73]

Certainly, this routine continued even in Metiaburj. 'A pulau as rich and nutritious as this used to be cooked every day for Wajid Ali Shah's principal wife.'[74]

Lucknow had been very distinct in its culinary practices, with an emphasis on flavour and painstaking cooking techniques. If pulao takes a big share of applause, then it must be noted that the quormas and kebabs of Lucknow were no less in their labour of love.

Referring to quormas, Collingham notes:

> In Lucknow, the Mughlai cuisine was transformed by the incorporation of the products of lush agricultural region of Oudh. The Lucknavis loved cream, and in the

eighteenth century used it to perfect the Mughal dish qauarama or what we would call korma. Qauarama was made only with the tenderest pieces of lamb or chicken and the name referred to the cooking technique of gently braising the meat in oil. Under the Mughals, the Persian method was applied, first marinating the meat in yogurt with ginger, garlic, onions and spices before simmering it gently in the yogurt sauce. The mixture was thickened with ground almonds, another Persian trick. In Lucknow, they added large dollops of cream to the sauce to create a dish [that] was voluptuously rich.[75]

Clotted cream locally called 'balai' was amply available. Indeed a unique name given by Nawab Asaf-ud-Daula for what is commonly known as malai. The word 'balai' is derived from the Persian word 'bala' (meaning 'above'), as the cream is actually extracted from the top layer of the milk. Even today, many would address malai as balai and vouch for its delicious taste.

Another unique ingredient is sattu or powdered Bengal gram, which has been used as an ingredient for a type of kebab called kachche tikia ke kebab. Sattu otherwise had been a traditional coolant made during the treacherously humid summers of Bengal, Bihar and Uttar Pradesh. When used in kebab, the kebab turns out lighter and more tender, and also fortifies it with a good amount of fibre, making it easily digestible. This was yet again a result of the continuous experiments by the rakabdars of the royal kitchen primarily for the ageing Nawab. Sattu, till today, is used in various signature kebabs of Lucknow like the galaouti kebab or pasanda.

Like moti pulao, galaouti, too, is symbolic of Awadhi cuisine, a star in the kebab category. Both are believed to have been

some disappeared because of the city's resistance to meaty dishes and some because the later chefs cooked commercially and didn't care much about the subtlety of the recipe.

While biryani still tops the list of favourites, a pride of the city, other delectables like rezala and seekh kebabs are favoured, too. On the contrary, nihari (the breakfast dish made of shanks of beef or lamb) or galaouti doesn't hold much emotion for Bengalis. Interestingly, the genesis of nihari lies in Old Delhi, or Purani Dilli, once known as Shahjahanabad, and not Lucknow.

To think of it, it would be quite a brave act for Bengalis to start their day with an audaciously meaty dish floating in a succulent thin, rich gravy, topped with finely chopped green chillies and julienned ginger, or even a dish like mutanjan, a sweet rice dish that clashed with the understanding of a typical mithai or dessert.

Curiously, the most familiar pulao with a distinct sweet note, including mutanjan, which every Bengali household claims as being handed down through family recipe, is in reality, a hybrid of several versions and renditions of the Lucknowi pulao but bereft of its subtlety.

Last but not least are the Awadhi breads and the puddings shirmal and shahi tukda, which remained burdened by their Muslim identity and had failed to make any connect with the Hindu Bengalis; a contradiction to Kolkata's love for mutton biryani and kathi rolls, which are equally Muslim, if we were to get down to that.

However, in the context of acquired tastes, the argument is that the Bengali middle class's and elite's leaning is towards English desserts, puddings and plum cakes rather than a shahi tukda, which nevertheless is also a bread pudding and of a finer palatability. The colonized mind was ready to open up to British tastes without questioning the Mughlai-elided Lucknowi desserts.

And yet, ironically, it is the generic 'Mughlai' food that works magic while ordering a meal at a restaurant.

PIT STOPS: SNACKING HOURS

For the settlers, the idea was to recreate a life that they had lived in England, and thus they celebrated visiting punch houses and theatres, racing on the Hooghly, and participating in boat and garden excursion, charities and dignity balls. The common thread among all these public amusement activities being food.

The Jockey Club was one of the earliest of its kinds, located at the erstwhile Loll Bazaar, or present-day Lal Bazaar, with an adjoining refreshment room that had a unique British name, 'Bread and Cheese Bungalow' and 'was at the far end of Bow Bazar, and in 1776 at the height of its popularity'.[77]

Here, on Sundays or holidays, the jockeys and amateur hunters would drop by for refreshments and then proceed for a hunting session to Dum Dum—the last limit of the city, a forest area with wild animals.

The British also brought their love for picnics to Calcutta and these were held in many locations including the Botanical Gardens, three miles away from the city limits on another end. The menu for these picnics always included eggs, hams, savoury omelettes, sandwiches, beef steaks and caramel custard. While beef steak and ham are still personal choices and could never find a place in the altered Bengali taste, omelettes, sandwiches and custards found their hold on Calcutta en masse.

It is hard to imagine now that Calcutta's beef was famous once. The city in fact had dedicated steak houses in the 1800s, proving to be a delight for the beef-loving Americans, many of whom were sailors surviving on salted beef through the long, perilous sea voyages, arriving at Calcutta with containers filled with ice.

In *Culinary Jottings*, one of the most popular cookbooks of the time, which ran into its fifth edition and was written by a British soldier, an author named Arthur Robert Kenney-Herbert (better known by his nom de plume 'Wyvern') on food and kitchen management in India, the omellete's indispensability is evident. He confesses, 'There is another source of satisfaction in our musing, and that is, that with moderate forethought we ought never to be unable to make a good savoury omelette, whether in camp, at a traveller's bungalow, at a picnic, or in the privacy of our back verandah in cantonment.'[78] 'Omelettes, as you all know, can be diversified ad libitum: we need never, therefore, be afraid of falling back upon them.'[79]

On the lines of the Bread and Cheese Bungalow, another petite refreshment room came up at Eden Gardens, Calcutta, which was designed by Emily Eden and her sister Fanny, once their loving brother Lord Auckland took on his role as the viceroy of India. This was an idea for a pit stop after a stroll at the Gardens, a much-needed one for the firangs, who were already used to their share of *chota hazri* (meal served shortly after dawn), burrah khana and tiffin.

By the early nineteenth century, Calcutta's first social club surfaced. Initially, it was called the United Service Club, which later was rechristened The Bengal Club, continuing even today. 'After Indian independence in 1947, the self-contained world of Anglo India was maintained among the British businessmen who "stayed on". Club life continued, cucumber sandwiches and sponge cake were served at tennis parties, and savouries still appeared at dinner parties.'[80] The menu of Bengal Club has retained its cucumber sandwiches, vegetable cutlets, chicken dopyazzas and orange soufflé, and their likes even today.

Ingredients and dishes that I have mentioned were getting introduced to the Bengali palette all this while. Their list is rather long but worth mentioning. In no specific order, they would consist of eggs, breads, biscuits, toasts, tea, fowl cutlets, chops, curries, mutton quorma, mutton biryani, chicken dopyazzas, pickles, oysters, condensed milk, cakes, puddings, soufflés, potatoes, carrots, cauliflower, cabbage, green peas, cloves, cardamoms, black pepper, bay leaves, saffron, tomatoes, long-grained rice, dry fruits, pineapples, raspberries, strawberries, wines and spirits. Their entry into Bengali kitchens manned by the women of the house were promoted by a multitude of cookbooks and women's magazines. Soon, every new vegetable and fruit, spices and condiments found their ground in the Bengali pantry.

Towards the beginning of the twentieth century, as public spaces like railway stations, universities, colleges, theatre halls, all-day dinings, canteens, restaurants, pice hotels and coffee houses opened up for most Indians, recipes made their way into the public domain. They became massy, popular and were carefully recrafted. By now, Bengalis have been drawn into snacking, both from the nutritive point of view and also as an act of social engagement, which is quite well-represented in various Bengali detective stories. In fact, serving Anglo-Indian snacks, such as the various chops and fries, to clients seems, more often than not, a way of prefiguring the 'progressive' template of the detective's modus operandi. So much so that 'the people of Calcutta turned their snacking into a fine art'.[81]

With British officials now returning and the untimely death of Nawab Wajid Ali Shah, a substantial number of cooks and their associates were left jobless. This skilled labour force, including the rakabdars, bawarchis, aubdars, khansamas, orderlies, *huccabardars* (carrier of hookahs) and caretakers, secured new employments, getting co-opted in public eateries and hotels. Some even started their own enterprises. Calcutta by then was relishing new food like toasts, tea, omelletes (with the easy availability of eggs), loaves and a tin of biscuits. It would not be long before these elements would make themselves integral to the new middle-class kitchen, going beyond exotic food experiments or replicating the forbidden pleasures of the outdoors.

3

Guava Jelly, or the Good Housekeeper Code

A debate sparked off around a recipe of guava jelly between two women's periodicals, namely *Antahpur* and *Punya,* at the start of the twentieth century. Utsa Ray describes this debate:

Antahpur first published a recipe for making guava jelly in January 1901. According to this recipe, the guavas first needed to be skinned and boiled for a while, then strained to get rid of the seed. The guava pulp was then to be mixed with sugar, constantly being stirred in the process. When the mixture thickened and have come to a room temperature, it could be bottled as guava jelly. This recipe was criticized by *Punya* in its January issue itself. The main critique was that the recipe given in *Antahpur* was picked from some other recipe book and not self-tried.[1]

While the debate centred around whose recipe was more authentic, it also marked a watershed moment in the popularization of new food like guava and its derivative jelly, letting them step inside Bengali households. The agenda of creating familiarity with ingredients hitherto unknown would be assigned to the young *bou* (newly married bride), who was expected of such an ask, like preparing guava jelly.

The expectations were neither one-off nor few but rather tall. Fulfilling them meant casting oneself in a full-time role of a sugrihini, conversant with home management, skillful in keeping track of monthly expenses, taking care of the husband, children and in-laws, maintaining the look of the house, nursing the ailing and, most definitely, cooking for her loved ones (read family). It wasn't enough to be an English-educated woman. One had to act beyond the purview of bookish knowledge and be dolled up as an 'ideal' woman, just like her Victorian counterpart, on whom the concept of a good housekeeper was based. In this context, Meredith Borthwick's research explains how Bengali words like 'sugrihini' was loaded, being interpreted in more ways than one,

> The sugrihini, or good housewife, was presented as an ideal in all literature directed towards women. She was one who toiled ceaselessly from morning till night, delighting in such labour. She was mindful of others' comfort and not preoccupied with her own… hospitable and generous without being extravagant, skilled in the culinary and medicinal arts and able to control a large household.[2]

English-educated Bengali women who went to school or were privately tutored, learning cookery as a subject, were thought to be inept when it came to actual cooking. Despite this critic, several women engaged in trying out new recipes, carrying out a meticulous pantry management. Borthwick further elaborates:

> In the traditional family structure, the *ginni* [older woman] was responsible for household organization. It was not to her, however, but to younger women who may have been setting up their own homes, or marking out their own domain in a larger household, that all the household manuals and magazine articles on domestic organization were addressed.[3]

With the advent of the printing press, there was an abundance of instructional domestic manuals and cookbooks. Surprisingly, nearly all the content in both categories were targeted to *nabinas* (younger women) and not *prachinas/ginnis* (mothers-in-law).

Griha Dharma, published in 1916, was written by reformist, educationist and Brahmo leader Shibnath Shastri and revolved around definitions of an ideal family, marriage and conjugal life. The book also includes a chapter on the rights of women in household matters. Around the same time, a host of articles across women's periodicals, such as *Bamabodhini Patrika, Antahpur, Punya, Bangalakshmi, Bangamahila, Paricharika* and *Abalabandhab* dished out clear mandates on the dos and don'ts for Bengali women.

It would be interesting to share here an extract from *Grihadharmma*—a similar manual, a namesake of Shastri's book authored by one Priyanath Basu in 1936—emphasizing the immense importance of the kitchen and pantry management: 'The wife or the good housekeeper's obligation as well as responsibilities are two pronged as she runs the family. One would be rearing the children and other would be to take care of the nutritive aspect of all other family members, facilitate a healthy life for them.'[4] Furthering the responsibilities, the manual holds her responsible if she is unable to offer a snack of some puri-sabzi and halwa on the sudden arrival of a guest.[5]

With instructions on how to be ever ready in her superwoman avatar, these periodicals and cookbooks provoked both elite and middle-class women compelling them to look at food preparation in a different light. It was a role they fancied playing with some quotient of duty and pleasure entwined, which would eventually lead to the emergence of new Bengali cuisine.

Ray writes:

There was a sea change in the material culture of colonial Bengali middle-class from mid-nineteenth century onwards which defined their habitus. Development of new restaurants enabled the middle class to experience 'new' food in a new environ while increase in the production of cookbooks fueled by print medium ensured that 'exotic' cuisine also became possible at home.[6]

Traditionally, the women of Bengal learned cooking from their mothers or the elderly women of the family, often helping them in kitchen activities. Sometimes, their learning adhered to the do-it-yourself (DIY) mechanics of today, as they stepped into the role of a miniature ginni equipped with their *khelnabati* (doll's house). Or, one of the many scenarios in a child's play would be enacting *ranna-bati* (the cookery play). Much later, in Satyajit Ray's *Pather Panchali* (1955), Durga, a teenage village girl, is shown playing the game of cookery with miniature mud ovens and utility wares.

For girls to get trained in cooking and learning to manage the kitchen were considered 'natural' and important as their other 'feminine' skills, namely sewing or taking care of the family elders. These skills were imparted mostly at the girl's natal home, and sometimes at her in-laws; some even learnt it the hard way, like Rassundari Devi—the earliest published woman writer from undivided Bengal and also the first Bengali author to have penned an autobiography.

In *Amar Jibon*, published in 1876 and reprinted in 1897, Rassundari Devi deliberates about her life as a 14-year-old, compelled to take over as a ginni or lady of the house once her mother-in-law lost her vision. In her candidly written autobiography, she talks of kitchen errands and cooking, amongst other aspects of her daily routine. A daughter-in-law, a wife and the mother of 12 children, Devi's autobiography is an eye-opener in understanding the lives of Hindu girls married young. She states, 'My day would begin at dawn and

I worked till two at night... I was fourteen years old... I longed to read books... But I was unlucky, those days women were not allowed to read.'[7]

In *Hindu Wife, Hindu Nation*, historian Tanika Sarkar remarks: 'These are some important words and themes from *Amar Jibon*, the first autobiography written by a Bengali woman and very probably the first full scale autobiography in Bengali language.'[8]

She further notes,

> At fourteen Rashsundari was looking after the entire household without any help. Her world was the kitchen and her 'cage' had distinct spatial connotations. She was in charge of the many ritual requirements of the family idol, she nursed her mother-in-law, looked after a stream of unexpected guests and cooked two meals every day for at least twenty-five people.[9]

Rassundari Devi could fit into the definitive sugrihini of the manuals, but in reality, her immensely challenging life was burdened with codebook expectations. For the earliest recorded Bengali woman writer, life was laborious and the lone respite came from being able to recite the *Chaitanya Bhagavat*[10], which she did discreetly.

Based in the remote Faridpur district of undivided Bengal, Rassundari Devi was deprived of formal schooling, which had already begun transforming the lives of women in Calcutta. Education for girls began during the mid-eighteenth century, overcoming huge resistance from orthodox quarters across class and religion. Interestingly, before the first school of Greater Calcutta saw the light of day, a handful of Brahmo families had already introduced their girls to education by home tutoring their daughters and wives, who were coached exclusively by European female teachers. In 1847, the first all-girls' school of Bengal started in Barasat and in the next two years, by the summer of 1849, Calcutta Female School (now known as Bethune School, the city's oldest girls' school) was founded by John Elliot Drinkwater Bethune, an English educator and polyglot.

Initial enrolment of students was sparse. Girls who finally ended up taking admission and attending classes followed strict purdah for commuting to school, using fully covered carriages or palanquins. Bethune, in his founding lecture, stated the need of 'educated mothers' who, would in turn, help build a 'civilized nation'. This was also the predominantly driving thought of all pro-British Bengali intelligentsia in favour of female education. Bethune sought their support to keep the school going, via routing a letter to Governor General Lord Dalhousie.[11]

Young women were trained afresh in those traditional skills, which they never knew had a method to them. Meredith Borthwick writes: 'Apart from more general subjects, girls were also going to learn "a thousand feminine works and accomplishments" in embroidery, fancy work and drawing, to give them a "means of adorning their own homes, and of supplying themselves with harmless and elegant employment".'[12] Cooking was one of them. 'There were calls for cooking to become part of the school curriculum for girls, thus institutionalizing the transmission of a traditional domestic ability. Schools in Bengal were urged to follow the precedent of some schools in England, where cooking had already been added to the curriculum.[13]

Recommendations from England were seriously taken back

home. In the growing milieu of women's education, culinary as a subject found its importance. In Ray's words:

> Schools like the *Uttarparah Hitkari* Sabha included cooking in its list of subjects for the study and a cooking prize was awarded by Madhya Bangla Sammilani. The Mahakali Pathshala, established on conservative Hindu principles in the year 1893, placed great emphasis on the learning of culinary skills. Even in the so-called modern educational institutions like the Victoria College, cookery was included in the curriculum.[14]

Other than curriculums at schools, magazines, too, played a big role in promoting cooking as a desirable act. I am not surprised though. My recall of high-school days does include omnipresence of women's magazine like *Sananda* and *Manorama* in many households of my neighbourhood and how women were smitten by their cookery columns.

Borthwick simply puts it in a historical timeline:

> A writer in the *Bamabodhini Patrika* of 1874 enumerated the types of cooking a *bhadramahila* should learn: native Brahmin dishes of rice and curry; meat in the Moghul style; sweetmeats made from chana, coconut, semolina, lentils, pumpkin and thickened milk; western style pickles and jams, cakes, biscuits, puddings and bread, and Indian roti, *luchi* and *puri*.[15]

They were also expected to know how to prepare special diets for children, nursing mothers and the differently abled—the latter included broths of sagu, arrowroot, barley and Benger's Food. The range of culinary learnings was assorted, hand-picked from cuisines of the Mughals, the English, the French and the Europeans at large. It's interesting to note the ease with which new dishes such as puddings, cakes and meat-based delicacies, hitherto unknown, were included. Cross-pollination was taking place in the repertoire of Bengali cooking. To that, there were direct references of the 'wishlist' dishes that all newly married women were expected to know, along with the statutory warning that they should be strictly prepared by the wife herself, instead of relying on helping hands or hired cooks.

Several essays written by both married and unmarried women were getting published in the columns of *Bamabodhini Patrika*. One of them carried in the October issue of 1882 titled 'Grihini', written by an anonymous author, who addressed herself as 'Sri', states,

> If the wife herself is not enough skilled in cooking, she must then keep a vigilant supervision on the cooks at her kitchen. Some of the wives are too lazy to even step into the kitchen. Although she might have access to a host of helping hands, it is her duty to step into the kitchen, monitoring the timely preparation of the meal. Some of them also have no dearth of ingredients in their pantry, it's just that the skill to prepare a fine meal is missing. If ever the man of the house would request for a special dish, the lazy wives surely would pass on the request, ordering the hired cook and get busy entertaining herself. Finally when lunch hour would approach and the husband was ready to savour a good meal, it would dawn upon her that the lunch isn't prepared, with some of the dishes still half cooked, some over-salted and others haven't made yet to the actual cooking stage.[16]

There is an evident glorification of 'womanly attributes' (read culinary skills) in these sentences. For the woman of the house, cooking for her husband and children was denoted as a sign of her 'labour of love', befitting her feminine, motherly instincts. In reality, the drudgery of routine cooking was a part of a Bengali woman's life for that is what they were socially conditioned to do. Only occasionally were they enamoured by the pleasures of learning new recipes.

In her memoir, *Chelebelar Dinguli* (The Childhood Days), Punyalata Chakraborty, who was born and raised in Calcutta of the 1880s in one of the most illustrious families (same as Satyajit Ray, the filmmaker), gives a detailed account of the joy of learning to cook. An observant, vibrant commentary on contemporary Bengali life, *Chelebelar Dinguli* describes her girlhood and her relationship with her mother, brothers and grandmother.

> My mother was a wonderful cook and knew a variety of dishes. Whenever she came across a new recipe, she would quickly pick it up. Sometimes she would innovate and create her own recipes. Throughout the year she would make a variety of jams, jellies, *murrabas* (fruit conserves) and distribute them to many relatives. Our home always had guests coming in. One day famed author Dr. J.T. Sunderland (author of *India in Bondage*) came over for a dinner. He was very impressed with the meal that my mother had served him. He remarked, 'If you come to our country (America) and open a school for cookery, I am sure it would be soon very famous and popular.'[17]

Punyalata's narrative reflected her mother Bidhumukhi's passion for cooking and experimenting with new food—a representation of some elite women. In the same breath, the author remarks how her mother never discriminated between her as a girl-child, getting her sons to learn kitchen skills as well.

Reminiscing about her childhood, she writes:

> Sometime while the family meal was cooked, my mother would often give us a little of those ingredients to create miniature versions of what was being cooked for the actual lunch. So I learnt to make *luchis* and made tiny '*luchis*' in tiny utensils, an exact replica of what my mother made but in a playful way.[18]

The *ranna-bati* way of course!

Punyalata's memoir is fascinating in very many ways. Not only did it reflect on different aspects of her girlhood, schooling and mother–daughter relationship, it also describes the city's evolving life, new food order, what entertainment was like in those days, along with impressions of her family members, who had left an indelible mark on her. In a thrilled tone, the writer details the celebratory mood of the family after Kadambini Ganguly, her maternal grandmother, returns from England post achieving her degree in medicine.

Kadambini Ganguly was the first Bengali woman to earn a Bachelor of Arts degree followed by her medicine degree—one of the earliest women to do so from all of British Empire. She travelled to Edinburgh for her higher studies. Punyalata mentions, 'After grandmother was back, her drawing room was rehauled, it wore a completely new look, the interiors were done with beautiful artistic objects and memorabilia that she had brought from England.'[19]

There a sense of freedom and individuality in this description, though the same cannot be vouched for the majority of Bengali women. Kadambini's case was an exception that only privileged families could foster, where men acknowledged the need for female education.

Another story of liberated female life was of Kailashbasini Devi, who became literate post her marriage with Durga Charan Gupta, a publisher. Her husband became her teacher. Later, she went on to publish her series of essays titled *Hindu Mahilaganer Heenabastha* (1863) on topics such as child marriage, female education, domestic labour and Hinduism. In two years, she wrote another book titled *Hindu Female Education and Its Progress* (1865), in which 'she expressed the opinion that most *madhyabitta grihastha* (middle-class householders) in the early part of the century saw no need for female education, but that the extension of British rule meant that this was no longer the case'.[20]

It is another matter that both families cited were Brahmos and had chosen to break away from mainstream Hinduism at that point.

In this exercise of literacy, cookbooks played a crucial role. The womenfolk favoured them for more reasons than one; sometimes owing to peer-pressured learning, occasionally to feel good about their newly acquired skills of being able to rustle up recipes from these books and on other instance, it was to declare their acceptance of modernity adding to self-fashioning.

Thus, dishes hitherto unknown started crossing over to household kitchens. An accidental snacking at an eatery or at a local moira could propel the idea of replicating them at home. Frequently referred were luchi, murraba pudding, cutlets, chops and various other sweetmeats. Bengalis found a sort of connect with snacking and these quick bites soon captured their collective imagination.

In *Chelebelar Dinguli,* Punyalata mentions a few of these sought-after bites, which she chanced upon on her way to school or at a moira.[21]

Luchi and sandesh were a must in a customary snack platter, which a young wife had to know how to make and serve in no time on the arrival of an unannounced guest. Their inclusion in recipe books and festivities such as weddings, Durga Puja and Maghotsav (Brahmo Festival) indicates a change in the eating habits of Bengalis. Much later, fictional characters of popular Bengali detective novels, sleuths like Feluda, Byomkesh, Bimal and his assistant Kumar and even funny, comic characters like Tenida were characterized by their favourite foods, which included cha, luchi, singara, ghughni (a snack made of chickpeas) and, of course sandesh and roshogolla.

Food and adventure went well together. I find cultural historian Tapati Guha-Thakurta's observations in this context brilliant. She writes:

It is worth noting here that the Bengali fascination with snacking, both as a nutritive and social act, is quite well-represented in various Bengali detective-stories. In fact, serving Anglo-Indian snacks—the various 'chops' and 'fries'—to clients seems, more often than not, a way of prefiguring the 'progressive' template of the detective's *modus operandi.* So much so that 'the people of Calcutta turned their snacking into a fine art'.[22]

In one of the stories with detective Byomkesh Bakshi, or the 'truth-seeker', as he liked to be called, one of the main characters, Debashish, is described as eating puris, which are similar to luchis, potato curry and home-made sweets.

In the 1940s, Narayan Ganguly (Gangopadhyay), a

well-known Bengali author, drew his unforgettable Teni da and his three sidekicks, all foodies, from real life. Ganguly had moved into a rented house in north Calcutta's Pataldanga area in 1946 and his houseowner's nickname was Teni. Later, when the idea of the first-ever Teni da story matured, Ganguly added on the delightful mania of new food to his hilarious characterization. Through his fun-filled novels, Teni da appeared as slightly bossy but a good-hearted, lazy fellow who is always munching on lip-smacking snacks of chops, cutlets, omelettes, singaras and what not!

Pyalaram, the meekest of Teni da's four-member gang, who is also the narrator of Teni da's stories, is portrayed as the quintessential middle-class man with chronic stomach ailments, heavily reliant on home-made remedies like potol diye singhi maacher jhol (catfish curry with pointed gourd) and bashok patar rosh (extracted juice of Malabar leaf). Fascinatingly, food remains a constant reference for both crime and comic storytelling.

By the beginning of the twentieth century, delight and enthusiasm around new foods—an impact of colonialism—held its sway, en masse. However, this new food was appropriated within the fold of domestic cuisine in Bengali homes. Cookbooks written in Bengali helped this appropriation, introducing a world of food preparations, often situating cooking as a type of recreation.

There was also a huge shift in tastes, habits and choices, which would go on to alter what was prepared within the four walls of the kitchens and served on plates, as well as how Bengalis of Calcutta would be known to the world in times to come.

In the 1830s, an interesting collaboration was being worked out between three men of Burdwan and Calcutta, resulting in an oddball venture. The said men were the Maharaja of Burdwan His Highness Mahtab Chand Rai (also known as Chuni Lal Kapoor), who had an ancestry of Lahore and was a connoisseur of art and education, as well as their funder; the second, a Bengali man named Bipradas Mukhopadhyay, who was a writer, editor and a food enthusiast with a pedagogic mind; and the third, a businessman and publisher who owned a printing press called Nitrayalal Sil. Together, they published the first-ever cookbook of India and the first one written in Bengali called *Pakrajeshwar* in 1831. This was the beginning of cookbooks followed by many more. The speciality of *Pakrajeshwar* was not only its recipes but also the listing of ingredients used along with a description of their health benefits—all in a compendium format.

'Cookbooks, which usually belong to the humble literature of complex civilizations, tell unusual cultural tales,' states anthropologist Arjun Appadurai.[23] His statement fits snug for Bengali cookbooks that were getting published in Calcutta, with *Pakrajeshwar* as the torchbearer.

By 1858, Mukhopadhyay's second book titled *Byanjon Ratnakar* was out. His books were groundbreakers, timed well, for there were no references of modern cookbooks written in Bengali other than the intermittent depictions of everyday life, and some impressions of eating habits and local produce in *Chandimangal* and *Annadamangal*. These eulogy literatures threw some light on what was eaten by Bengal's caste-conscious society. There was the indigenous hunter-gatherer couple Kalketu and Phullara, and Lahana and Khullana, who were the two wives of the affluent merchant called Dhanapati—all characters from *Chandimangal*. While Kalketu and Phullara's meals consisted of their unsold hunt proceeds like boars and porcupine, the merchant family ate elaborate, hearty meals of fish, vegetables and dairy. A more recent *Mangal Kabyo, Annadamangal* was more adventurous in its depiction of food and mentions tortoise eggs and dried fish, which in the nineteenth century were considered blasphemous by the upper-caste Hindu Bengalis.

Medieval *Mangal Kabyo* texts are not adequate referrals. To understand what Bengalis ate, one needs to fall back on cookbooks written over the last two centuries. 'The proliferation of presses, journals, and books in the nineteenth-century colonial context did, among other things, usher in the prototypes of the modern cookbook.'[24]

Even though the modern-day cookbook *Pakrajeshwar* had a second edition, there was a long gap of 27 years between Mukhopadhyay's two publications. Mukhopadhyay was heavily influenced by multiple textual sources, from the ancient Indian cooking manual called *Ksemakutuhalam* by Khsemsharma, who was employed in the court of King Vikramaditya, to Puranic references, to the Mughal cookbook called *Nuskha-i-Shahjahani*, written during Shah Jahan's regime. 'In 1889, Bipradas Mukhopadhyay brought out *Soukhin-khadya-pak* part one, which included instructions on the cooking of kheoarccnna (rice, lentils, spices and fat), khichudi pullao, rich curry, korma, shishkebab, kofta, cutlets and chops. Part two included English food.'[25]

The two volumes were then collated to publish *Pak Pranali* in 1906, which also included some recipes from the namesake monthly magazine which Mukhopadhyay edited.

Pak Pranali turned out to be his most significant work. The singular effort with which Mukhopadhyay advocated renewed culinary learning was remarkable, all the while emphasizing modernity (read contemporariness). In *Pak Pranali,* he creates a mind-boggling world of recipes. Shifting from refined Bangla, these recipes were written in a simpler version of the vernacular.

Even before one leafs through the recipe section, the 'Introduction' bares open Mukhopadhyay's idea of good food, which is always nutritive and one made with care. The opening disclaimer compares the mortal Bengali wives and mothers with the Hindu goddess of food, Devi Annapurna (Lord Shiva's wife). The author is upfront about his preference for food being cooked at home and states that there is substitute for good home-cooked food. He harps on how satisfying it is for a woman to cook for her husband and children, who would always be looking for her caring touch in all the meals that were served.[26] Spread over 16 chapters, the introductory one begins with a discussion on the ideal kitchen and pantry as well as their upkeep. Insisting on an airy, well-lit pantry, the author emphasizes on strict cleanliness. He also doles out useful tips such as frequent dusting and the occasional sunbathing of the reserve grains as well as of the pickles and ghee, which would eventually help keep the pantry hygienic and pest-free.

The kitchen management segment in Bipradas Mukhopadhyay's book is inspired from the English (read scientific) way of life. Meredith Borthwick writes in *Shadow or Substance*: 'Women carried out the daily domestic routine within the *antahpur,* an inner courtyard surrounded by a kitchen and living apartments. The male recreation and reception area was located beyond this, around an outer courtyard from which there was access to the public street.'[27] She adds: 'Although the outer apartments were usually reasonably commodious and airy, the *antahpur* was dingy. Cooking-rooms without proper chimneys, and smoky outlets generally, form part of these dwelling apartments.'[28]

For the more affluent families, there were rooftops, often the only source of unhindered sunlight. It was in this lone open space that women stole their moments of gossip and pastime. The imperative of keeping a kitchen and pantry clean and well-lit advocated by Mukhopadhyay perhaps finds a rationale.

Further in the book, he chooses to list all the vegetables and spices that were used frequently and enumerates more than 200 recipes. With each entry, the author comments on the nutritive and therapeutic aspects of these ingredients, referring to Ayurvedic texts tagged as Vaidya Shastra. Interestingly, the list of vegetables in *Pak Pranali* begins with potatoes. The author appears to favour potatoes, recognizing the heightened lusciousness it brings to some fish- and meat-based recipes when potentially combined. The reader is instructed to retain the potato skin while boiling, as that would be a healthier way to preserve its nutritive values. Note that this was the year 1906 and potatoes were gaining popularity along with other 'new' vegetables like cabbages, cauliflowers, tomatoes, peas and carrots. The sheer size of entries under 'potato' shows how important it already was, when compared to other vegetables like carrots, cabbages and cauliflowers. He was fairly dismissive of both their taste and functionality, like his earlier comment on carrot, labelling them high on water content and low on nutrition. The cruciferous vegetables only got themselves a minor brownie point.

Bipradas Mukhopadhyay hails onions and also includes garlic in this list but with a caveat. While onion gets his vote for being a versatile ingredient, being recommended as a 'must' for cooking mutton dishes, garlic is scorned off. Additionally, he describes the benefits of onion as anti-cough and cold, sperm-inducing and beneficial in pain management. Though garlic makes it to his list, it is negatively associated because of its pungency and is slapped by a strong casteist remark, which in sum means 'prolong usage of garlic in cooking would make one loose one's (jaat/caste and dharma/faith) and have foul smell in their pee and poop. He states that it is pungency of the garlic which forbade the Hindus to use it at all'.[29] In some instances, he dispenses the use of onions, too, like in the recipe of Mughlai khichudi included in the chapter dedicated to khecharanna—the now obsolete Sanskritized term for simply 'khichudi' or 'khichdi'.[30]

Mukhopadhyay was a clever man. He could sense his reader's mind, who mostly belonged to the upper caste and for whom onions and garlic were a no. Overtly vetoing these ingredients could mean a potential dip in Mukhopadhyay's readership. Nevertheless, he did stretch himself, trying to be inclusive. From boiled, baked, braised and deep fried dishes to dry, thin and thick curries, *Pak Pranali* did not leave any stone unturned in including various kinds of recipes. Just the sheer variety of recipes is unthinkable for a cookbook of 1906. Interestingly, Mukhopadhyay was later criticized by Nikhil Sarkar, aka Sripantho, who edited a contemporary volume of Bipradas Mukhopadhyay's first two books *Pakrajeshwar* and *Byanjon Ratnakar.* 'Sripantha who compiled and edited these two texts wrote in the introduction to the texts that the authors of these two recipe books drew heavily on the recipes from the Mughal period; they were definitely not writing a book of everyday Bengali recipes.'[31]

Calcutta on Your Plate

It is hard to say if Sripantha's critiques of Mukhopadhyay's first and second cookbooks were valid, as the editions had long been out of print. Not much is known about them, except *Pakrajeshwar*'s popularity in its second edition.

Mahatab Chand, Maharaja of Burdwan, funded the second edition while it was published by writer-journalist Gaurishankar Bhattacharya, also known as 'Gurgure' Bhattacharya. 'Gurgure' in Bangla means a roly-poly kid who often walks cutely. Surely, a food book publisher fits into this adorability. The book, printed in a press called Kalpadrum located at Mirzapur Street of Calcutta, was just about 93 pages. Reverend James Long, who was the first bibliographer of Bengali books, further notes Bipradas's inclusion of ancient recipes in the book as old as two millennia.

Borthwick mentions, 'The journal was illustrated, and recipes were clearly set out with a list of ingredients followed by the method, often giving a brief history of the dish as well.'[32]

Perhaps a reflection of Mukhopadhyay's clever and modern mind, *Pak Pranali* included several unexpected dishes: Jewish fish fry, an English chop, a Dawoodkhani khichdi, French lamb cutlet, pineapple pulao, a tangerine/orange pulao, Noormahali biryani, Arabic jasmine pulao, pishpash or mutton rice, mutton omelette, egg Mughlai kofta, Irish stew, orange jelly, half-boiled egg and lamb, mach bhaete (mashed fish), phoolkopi bhaete (mashed cauliflower), habshi pulao, prawn kofta curry, rohu English curry, hasty pudding, plum pudding, Chinese kebab (tiger prawns), Italian lamb pie, French potato chops, dilkosh dolma, fish dumpukht, cauliflower stew, German pudding, and many more. And all coexisted with the conventional Bengali platter of dal, bhaja and bhaté (boiled while the rice is being cooked or separately and then mashed with salt and condiments) or charchori (dishes made out of stems of various vegetables which are normally discarded).

Bipradas even tweaked traditional recipes, adding ingredients quite unthinkable. Like in the recipe of bhuni khichudi, usually a vegetarian dish, he added hilsa, a local fish. It became a new dish altogether—illish bhuni khichudi.

For later readers, the vast variety of recipes in *Pak Pranali* may appear a little randomly put together, but looking back, the inclusions reflect how Calcutta was, in the early twentieth century, negotiating its rising culinary hybridity—an indicator of its openness and cosmopolitanism that Bengalis were seemingly embracing. The inclusiveness of *Pak Pranali* was subtly spread out throughout the book. Soon, the impact of these books and his continuous food writing began to be noticed and acknowledged. Women began writing cookbooks. They started coming up with new recipes and even got those published in women's magazines more frequently than anyone expected.

The next in line of impactful cookbooks was a quirkily advertised book called *Pakprabandha* (Essays in Cooking), which appeared out of nowhere, taking the market by some intrigue. Cleverly promoted in *Indian Mirror*'s March 1879 issue, it read, '*Pakprabandha*, a Bengali book of "well-tried recipes for the preparation of rare and delicate Mahomedan, Hindu, and other dishes", by "a Bengali Lady" at a price of five annas in 1879.'[33]

This was surely an advertisement that would skewer the curiosity of readers about the identity of the author, as well as generate an eagerness to know about the food of the 'other'; recipes which were not their own. For the Hindus, it would mean Muslim recipes and for Muslims, the recipes of Hindus. As for the author's identity, she definitely wanted to remain anonymous. Not much is known about *Pakprabandha* beyond this. By 1907, the extremely influential *Amish O Niramish Ahaar* (Non-Vegetarian and Vegetarian Food), written by Pragyasundari Debi, came out in two volumes.

'Both Mukhopadhayay and Pragyasundari's cookbooks are classic examples of the changing diets of Bengalis,' remarks Utsa Ray.[34] But were the early authors writing for a wide spectrum of Bengali readers enabling their everyday cooking as well as helping them prepare 'specials'? I would say Mukhopadhyay was at it. He was liberal enough to goad his readers to try out recipes with new ingredients like oranges (orange kalia), pineapple (pineapple pulao), black cardamom (Noor-Jahani fish kebab) and the humble potato (potato cutlets).

The sudden emphasis on unknown vegetables, including potatoes, carrots, cabbages, cauliflowers and radishes, was sowed primarily as British experimentation in local agriculture—an important aspect of their colonization imbued with the 'desire to recreate a home-like situation in the colony'.[35]

Potato had been labelled as 'poor man's food' in England, but when it reached British colonies like India, it simply meant the introduction of new agricultural practices, recreating what England farmed. 'This attitude motivated the English to bring this experiment to India as well. A constant search for substitutes for rice led the colonial state to concentrate on the cultivation of potatoes and peas. Those who already sowed potato were asked to instruct others to sow it too.'[36] The hilly terrains of Bengal were suitable for cultivating potatoes, from where they were distributed to Calcutta and the rest of the state.

Though he created exotic recipes, experimental enough to raise inquisitiveness, Bipradas Mukhopadhyay was careful not to alienate his readers—the elite, middle- and upper-caste, educated women. That said, there was an elitist approach to what Mukhopadhyay offered, but it was never disconnected from the archaic Bengali understanding of food. If his readers tried only few of his eclectic recipes, for Mukhopadhyay, it would be closer to achieving his goal. And for him, the goal was to induct different platters representing various communities, drawn from a polyglot population of Calcutta. In sum, he was categorical in reviving the 'lost art' of Bengali cooking.

An example would be what he calls 'Hindostani arhar dal'. He goes about the recipe by stating how this dal often tastes more scrumptious when cooked by women living outside of Bengal, or *Paschim Desh*, which would mean any place up north. Then, he gets down to the list of ingredients needed, describing each step. The ingredients are pigeon split peas, coriander, cumin, green chilli, hing (asafoetida), turmeric, a slice of lemon and water. Note the use of hing. He impresses upon what a North Indian arhar dal recipe ideally would be, by adding a touch of a new spice (not familiar in Bengal) like asafoetida. The same dal when described as 'Badshahi arhar dal' included loads of ghee, yogurt, ginger, cinnamon, cardamom, cloves and zafran (saffron); clearly, a Mughal-influenced version with the different set of spices. Minute differences in recipes sometimes by a variation in spices or its omission and techniques of cooking, were good enough a provocation for an aspiring sugrihini to try out a new dish—an indicator of the balance that Bipradas Mukhopadhyay so excellently stroked.

Pragyasundari Devi, one of Tagore's nieces, authored more than a one-off *Amish O Niramish Ahar, Jarak* and *Randhan Rhahra* (in Assamese). While the second and third books are out of print, *Amish O Niramish Ahar* has held its ground even after 113 years, now considered a cult with many successful reprints. Pragyasundari also edited *Punya*, a family magazine published in the culturally stimulated environment of the Tagores between 1897 and 1902.

Punya was first published in 1897, and Pragyasundari herself wrote a statutory *Ganesha Vandana* (reverence of the Elephant god Ganesha) and then a descriptive version of how to offer reverence to one's ancestors, termed as *Pitritarpan,* before the first dish of the magazine. A dessert called chandrakana or chandrakanto mithai (a moon-shaped sweet) was discussed too. This was followed by a prawn cutlet recipe and a mutton liver do pyaza, passaging on to a poem on Goddess Durga.[37] Further, the first recipe in the second volume is called Vidyasagar barfi (a sweetmeat named after Ishwar Chandra Vidyasagar, the nineteenth-century Bengali reformer and educator), preceded by an essay on 'Spirituality and Aesthetics', as well as one on the 'Five Elements of Hindu Cosmology' or 'Panchabhoot' and then comes recipes of fish in mustard and dahi vada.[38]

It is interesting to observe how Pragyasundari created a narrative of culinary with roots in the Vedic Indian traditions, which she, like her predecessor Mukhopadhyay, considered as being 'lost in time' and thus must be reimagined and reconstructed. She paints an erstwhile glorious Bengal as well as Bharat (the land), laden with Aryan norms, where cooking had been an art but not bereft of practicality.

Reading her is fascinating. She does not take into account any of the later influences including the Mughals or the Europeans. The present edition of her voluminous *Amish O Niramish Ahar,* with 1,500 recipes, retains her original introduction, starting with the generic observances of any Hindu religious narrative. The lengthy introduction to the book concludes as:

> India is a repository of knowledge and there is no exception
> when it comes to knowledge of food, edibles. There is an
> artificial difference created between Hindus and others
> when it comes to gastronomy. The other populaces have
> followed the Hindus when it came to gastronomic affairs.
> The range of delicacies: be it from the Arabs, Persians or
> other Muslim countries or even Europe, where did they
> emerge from? Where did those communities learn it
> from? Of course they learnt from India.[39]

Curiously, the 'foreign' that she ruled out in her long
introduction, at the onset of her book, got incorporated
in her recipes amply in the name of innovation. In a brief
foreword to the current edition of *Amish O Niramish Ahar*,
Pragyasundari's granddaughter, Ira Ghosh, mentions how
prolific her grandmother was, 'It is believed that Pragya had
contributed to the creation of Icmic Cooker and Indubhushan
Mallick its creator, wanted to dedicate the patent to Pragya.
However she did not accept his offer.'[40] Even though she didn't
accept Mallick's offer, she was supportive of his invention.
The short endorsement welcoming the new concept of steam
pressure cooker read, 'This edition has many additional recipes,
and I have also included few recipes which are appropriate
to be cooked in Icmic cooker that is a creation of stalwart
Dr. Indumadhab Mallick.'[41]

Indumadhab Mallick, a scion of the Mallick family of
Bhowanipur, was a philosopher, physicist, physician, inventor,
entrepreneur, writer and social reformer. He created an
innovative tool—a steam cooker—in 1910 which would help
cut on cooking time. Icmic's easy technique and portability

made it a success and paved the way for home-cooker brands such as Santosh and Rukmini, among others, which were targeted at the aspiring middle class, whose lives needed a redefined time management.

Innovation was always acceptable for Pragyasundari and as a recipe developer, she innovated wonderfully with unheard-of ingredients. Her prawn cutlet recipe had fresh herbs like parsley and cilantro (alien to Bengal), and in her mushroom soup, she added canned meat to thicken the broth. For a French-sounding meal option called Blomas, meant for the unwell, Pragyasundari used arrowroot and cornflour. On the other hand, there were many examples of new vegetables such as potatoes, cabbages and tomatoes cooked in traditional Bengali style for vegetarian recipes. She also drew recipes from the European palette, which had names unmistakably resonating their origins, such as German soup, egg in sherry, duck egg escru, Curbin, Auf Asas, Kromosky, Pate D Pom Dete, Rolypoly pudding, Tipsy pudding and more.

While most of these dishes were truly of European origin, there were some dishes to which words such as 'firangi' or 'French' were intentionally added to heighten their exoticness. For example, firangi begun bhaja (firangi fried aubergine), French golaruti (golaruti being a local pancake) and Parisian chechki. Pragyasundari appears unhesitant in creating an assortment of recipes along with her regulars like variants of dals or bhajas, essentially more desi stuff.

In all the most significant of her reimaginations were rice dishes and sweets with a tweak: Rammohan dolma pulao, Dwarka Nath phirni pulao, Dwarka Nath motihaar, Vidyasagar barfi and kobi sangbardhana barfi (a special sweetmeat made of cauliflower commemorating the poet laureate Tagore's fiftieth birthday in 1911). Pragyasundari was asked to make something special for this celebratory occasion.

Describing her recipe of Rammohan dolma pulao, she stated that the dish is dedicated to the memory of reformer and educator Raja Rammohan Ray as well as mentions its literal name, mitha dolma pulao, but without referring to the Armenian connect with dolma.

Similarly, for the sweetmeat Vidyasagar barfi, there is a descriptive footnote that compares this innovative sweet with the existing pistachio barfi, appreciating how her creation is easy on the stomach and no less delicious than the latter.[42]

Pragyasundari's recipes ring in an interesting coexistence of the new food order with what has been prevailing. Constantly experimenting with ingredients, she played with genres, sometimes naming dishes rather quizzically, making it tricky to understand their cultural roots. For example, recipes like indral, ilisher ulhas, isafu, karan kuku, mutton birinchi, murgir hoteli pulao, pishpash with murgi, patoler fareta, deemer fifu, and so on.

While they may sound exotic, in reality, they were the result of experimentations that Pragyasundari did. In some of these recipes, she included the most unusual combinations, like in isafu, she added aubergine to prawns instead of ilish or hilsa, a traditional combination found in Bengal and in aloo mekhela, a name she devised for the conventional country captain, the hurriedly cooked poultry dish, mutton is substituted by chicken, and cooked with yogurt and other spices. In its original form, this is an 'on-the-go dish', something which the bawarchis at the dak bungalows rustled up with almost nothing but a hurriedly killed chicken.

In sum, Pragyasundari's cookbook, containing a variation of

as many as 80 dals and 40 ways of cooking rice, was distinct, with novelties and syncretic recipes. She was smart to game up the 'exotic', tantalizing the nomenclature of some generic categories like pulao. The innovations she conceived toed the lines of hybridity: a norm of the day. Amusingly, she mostly denied any cross-cultural influences; however, their abundant inclusion in a variety of recipes only proves otherwise. *Amish O Niramish Ahar* can be thus defined as a cookbook with an eclectic collection of recipes, a glimpse into the psyche of Calcutta's elite and the middle class at the turn of the twentieth century.

More cookbooks continued to be published, while women's magazines encouraged subscribers to send in their own recipes. Between 1901 and 1903, *Antahpur*, a monthly magazine, carried some very interesting recipes like pineapple jelly, custard apple malpua (a desi version of pancakes) and moong dal mohanbhog, among others. Jelly was never a local recipe, for there was no concept of a bread spread, neither was it considered a sweet dish. It was a direct British influence as was the pancake. Pineapple, too, was a new fruit. As for moong dal mohanbhog, it was a North Indian sweet delicacy and not a part of Bengal's existing repertoire of sweetmeats and desserts.[43] In no time, the very same desserts got included in wedding and party menus that affluent Bengalis hosted.

The above recipes are typical examples of contemporary cookbooks that were cross-culturally fuelled and pollinated during various regimes. Also, 'discussions on food was supplemented with information on the use of unan (mud oven) to create temperatures akin to those in Western-style ovens, along with information on the use of various utensils'.[44]

In an essay on 'Reading Women Through Their Recipes:

The Cookbooks of Bengal', scholar Rituparna Das mentions:

Binapani Mitra's *Cheleder Tiffin* [Tiffin for Children] came out in 1941. Introduced in the cover as 'Sahitya Saraswati' (Goddess of Literature), Mitra begins by stating [the] health benefits of consuming local foods as opposed to 'foreign food' such as cakes and biscuits. In the manner of a case study, she tells a story she heard from an old physician in Calcutta: A famous attorney, a relative of this physician, went to a cardiologist in Germany to get treated for his heart condition. The German cardiologist's breakfast spread, surprisingly, comprised the humble *muri* (puffed rice), *gur* (jaggery) and *peshai narkel* (grated coconut), eaten commonly in rural Bengal. It was supposedly this food that kept him in good shape. Binapani Mitra goes on to provide around a hundred-odd recipes that could be innovatively assembled using inexpensive local produce. Recipes for *kacha peper chop* (fritters made of green papaya), *chine badam barfi* (sweetmeat made of peanuts) and *ananda laddu* (sweet made of coconut, rice flour and sesame) were written with emphasis on their restorative qualities.[45]

Randhansanket, the other book written by Mitra, reflects a certain openness that the contemporary times called for.

Openness may be interpretational. For some, like Mitra and Bipradas Mukhopadhyay, ignoring what was commonly used, say, curry powder, was an expression of openness. Utsa Ray cites the seed of 'hybridity' here:

It needs to be mentioned that Mitra had curry recipes for fish like koi, which was only found in Bengal. However Mitra's koi curry did not contain the curry powder that was used in Anglo-Indian cuisine. She simply uses ground onion, ginger, turmeric, and ghee or clarified butter for the *koi* curry. Mitra's book had recipes for such hybrid food like 'khirer toffee' (thickened milk toffee).[46]

Reflection of this newness was best evident in the descriptions of jams, jellies, pickles and murabbas. Note that murrabas are fruit conserves commonly consumed in Azerbaijan, Armenia, Georgia, Persia, the Middle East, South Caucasus and Central Asia. While I have mentioned pineapple and guava jelly earlier, Snehlata Devi's *Achar O Murabba* (Pickles and Sweet Preserves) simply included gulkand (sometimes differently spelt as 'gulqand' or 'gulkhand'). Gulkand literally means 'gul' (rose) and 'kand' or 'khand', which is a sugary sweetish preserve with its origin in Persia, wherein Damask roses were exclusively used to make it finely fragrant. Although hard to trace when exactly it travelled to the subcontinent, gulkand had been a part of Unani medicine, known for its therapeutic qualities like enhancing eyesight and improving digestive system.

Renuka Devi Chaudhari's *Rakamari Amish Ranna* and *Rakamari Niramish Ranna* were published in two volumes in 1988 (after the author passed away). She was born in 1910, and detailed her experiences as a young wife and mother of the zamindar household of Muktagachha in the Mymensingh district of erstwhile East Bengal.

Married at the age of 10 and prodded into cooking by her father-in-law Raja Jagat Kishore Chaudhuri, Renuka Devi's book acknowledged influences from earlier writers like Pragyasundari Devi, while also including what was traditionally cooked at her home in Muktagachha. She owed much of her learnings to the itinerant bawarchis employed with the estate.

One Noora Bawarchi in particular, who happened to be the head cook, was a great influence on her.

Reminiscing about her life in an autobiographical essay, *Amar Katha* (My Story), she opens up about her culinary training and how over the years, she had collected recipes from friends and family resulting in the finality of her two-volume cookbook, containing 400 vegetarian and 300 non-vegetarian recipes. The non-vegetarian dishes listed have a host of uncommon roasts, kebabs and quormas made of deer meat, duck and pigeon meat. Renuka Devi categorizes them as influenced or adapted by the bawarchis. The index mentions them within brackets as examples of cross-cultural learnings. For example: bhaja rui-er French quorma (French quorma of fried rohu) was under the category 'Bawarchi Khana', while mangsher steak (meat steak) was under 'Bawarchi Pranali'.[47]

Syncretic element of Bengali cooking and its resultant hybridity is undeniable. Ray, in her *Culinary Culture in Colonial India*, emphatically notes this hybridity element:

> Hybridity became a frequent occurrence in the recipes we find in most of the Bengali periodicals that appeared around this time. Often a mutton chop recipe or a potato stew recipe contained ingredients like ghee or clarified butter, which [were] mostly used for Hindu ritual practices. The periodical Paricharika came with a recipe for a muffin made of potato and *patol* (pointed gourd: a very locally grown and locally consumed vegetable).[48]

A good mix-up leading to new epicurean habits was due to the availability of 'foreign' products, ingredients including various herbs, tea, coffee, canned food and condensed milk, among others. To familiarize one with these vegetables, herbs and any other ingredient, Pragyasundari wrote a footnote mentioning where they would be available and, in most cases, it would be Hogg Market or Terretti Bazaar. She also lent her insight on the market price of these ingredients and whether they were pocket friendly for the upper- and middle-class Bengalis.

By the mid-twentieth century, the vernacular publishing was full of utterly popular cookbooks written by Leela Mazumder, Bela De, Sadhana Mukhopadhyay, and their likes. Bela De's titles were mostly bestsellers, running into many editions, but like Renuka Devi, De wrote from her experiences of earlier times, filled with insights of Calcutta in the 1930s, '40s and later, by which time the 'foreign' was included in these books, repurposed as 'true' blue Bengali cookbooks.

De actually became quite a phenomenon beyond the realm of her writing, when she turned into a radio host for the popular women's programme called *Mahila Mahal* (The World of Women), aired by All India Radio's Calcutta unit. A generation still remembers *Mahila Mahal* with a lot of warmth, a sort of urban lore.

However, the contents of these books were expansive and unabashedly mixed up in their categorization. There would be a meat loaf addressed as mangsher ruti ('mangsho' in Bengali is meat and 'ruti' is the generic term for a flattened bread), which should ideally come under 'breads', penang chicken under Chinese food and a duck quorma ideally under Mughlai cuisine, all clubbed in one category as non-vegetarian.[49] Strangely, the diffusion of categories proved to be a reason for their popularity.

These cookbooks turned out to be social levellers unlike their earlier lot. Nearly every middle-class Bengali home owned more than one Bela De or Sadhana Mukhopadhyay title. De's books were much sought after. They even got pirated, resulting in low-quality publishing and noticeable errors in grammar and cooking terms.

THE FINAL MIX-UP: CHA, BISKOOT AND TELEBHAJA

With the availability of ingredients and a multitude of cookbooks, Bengali food was opening up, breaking free from informed imagination, becoming adaptable than before, gathering acceptance from a large segment of the population. Gautam Chakrabarti writes: 'From the end of the eighteenth century to that of the nineteenth and onwards, "some of the best-selling new products of the period—Mellin's and Lactogen's baby foods, Keventer's butter, Firpo's bread, Nestle's condensed milk, the all-time health drink, Horlicks [as well-received now as it was then], Coca Cola and Morton Sweets" were made available in Calcutta.'[50]

Some of the above-mentioned products that generations of Bengalis have grown up with are no longer available. Their initial foray into the city's markets lead to diverse culinary hybridization that would acquire a template of cosmopolitanism in Bengali food. As a school-going child, I had often heard women at home saying, '*New Market-e bagher dudh-o pawa jay*' (At New Market, even tiger milk is available). Note the word 'new', which captures the complete essence of culinary improvisation. In literal terms, it is the revamped name for Sir Stuart Hogg Market, the first municipal market of Calcutta thrown open for its English customers on 1 January 1874 and named Municipal Commissioner of Calcutta Hogg Saheb.

Chakrabarti adds:

Calcutta provided ample opportunity for its inhabitants to mediate their transition from a somewhat-liminal existence on the fringes of Hindustan to a suddenly-empowering situation as residents of a new transnational imperial capital, as it was destined to become by the end of the nineteenth century. As befitting their new-found status as residents of a global city that was roughly in the middle of East-West trade for a considerable amount of time and which traded with cities old and new, Calcuttans sought to broaden their culinary horizons.[51]

Fresh gastro pleasures perked up both home kitchens as well as public eateries. Tea was the most desired brew, while coffee was still predominantly an elite drink for the *bilet pherat*, or 'England returned'. Unknown but factual, Bengalis' love for coffee preceded their loyalties for tea, a much later phenomenon at the turn of the twentieth century. Bengal's coffee connect by then was 200 years old, started during the days of Bengal Nizamat when Behrampore in Murshidabad was the provincial capital. Coffee was a much-needed import for the Nawab Nazims of Murshidabad, an integral element of their fine living. This in turn would bring up the picture of consumption connected to the culture of the court described by Tilottama Mukherjee, an eighteenth-century Bengal/Medieval and Early Modern India historian:

> The court in Bengal as elsewhere, in the early modern period, in widely accepted definition was an arena of interface between the Nazims and other sections of society, 'a cultural trend setter', centre of patronage, focus of politics and the household of the ruler. Court culture included habits of consumptions, religious beliefs,

devotional practices, modes of dresses and other markers of status and function and patronage of arts.[52]

Alivardi Khan's court was no exception. A nuanced description of Alivardi emerges from the *Seir Mutaqherin* or Review of Modern Times (second volume), brilliantly written by historian Syed Gholam Hussein Khan, who was also the Nawab's cousin.

The character of Alivardi Khan (also spelt as Aaly Verdy Qhan in the original book) is rather interesting. A perceptive and shrewd man, Alivardi had fine tastes. He was a connoisseur of good food, witty conversations and Turkish coffee, which he meticulously consumed every day after Fajr namaz. He was also an ailurophile who loved Persian cats and sometimes participated in instructing his cooks as they prepared royal meals of the day. Gholam Hussein Khan writes, 'He always rose two hours before daylight; and after having gone through evacuations and ablutions, he performed some devotions of supererogation and at daybreak he said his prayers of divine precepts, and then drank coffee with choice friends.'[53] He further describes a highly refined milieu, typical of court cultures of the day:

After that he amused himself with a full hour of conversation, hearing verses, reading poetry or listening to some pleasing story; to which we must add occasional orders, which he would give about some dish or other, which was always dressed in his presence at that time to the care of which was appointed, either some of the persons then present, or some person freshly come from Persia or any other country renowned for good cookery; for he was fond of good eating, and had a taste very nice and very delicate.[54]

Calcutta on Your Plate

It might be a pleasant revelation for many that Bengal already had a caffeine affinity, manifested in its full-blown coffee culture, much before tea occupied their sensoria. Records tell that coffee was one of the oft-traded commodities that travelled from Central Asia and Turkey to Bengal. 'A steady stream of people as well as commodities whether poets and musicians, or goods such as silk, tobacco, coffee, spices, dyestuffs and textiles across Central Asia tied Mughal India to the Ottoman Empire through the larger part of seventeenth and eighteenth century.'[55] Further observations mention, 'The Nazim's household retained the services of a wide range of professional groups such as storytellers, painters, coffee makers, ice makers, *hakims* (physicians).'[56]

Such descriptive passages lead to imagining a Nizamat of fine court culture, epicurean and artistic in its nature. Consequently, it doesn't need much historical acumen to intuitively sense its designed fall in the near future. Luxurious courts tend to die faster, as history tells us.

Exactly at which juncture the coffee culture disappeared from the precolonial life of Bengal is hard to decipher, but presumably, it would be no later than 1757. Alivardi Khan had a mixed ancestry of Arab and Afshar Turkman; instinctively, coffee held a great importance for him. He was a disciplined man, yet a connoisseur of good life. Siraj ud-Daulah, his grandson and successor, was not a patch on him. The fine court culture was lost in no time as was the fate of Bengal.

By the first-half of the nineteenth century, cultivation of tea started both in Assam and Darjeeling. The next few decades also saw the emergence of public eateries, restaurants, cafés, coffee houses and railway canteens across the city. Drinking tea became widespread, it was available everywhere. Not only did it step into the inner fold of Bengali life, it also turned out to be a leveller going beyond class–caste, poor–rich divides, in the already stratified Calcutta.

Suddenly, almost everyone was cherishing a cup of tea.

Fascinatingly, it was not always enamouring between Bengalis and their cup of tea, or cha as they call it! Long after the British had invested in tea, growing it in the sleepy terrains of Darjeeling, Calcutta started taking notice of tea. The farming of the leaves was driven by British interests of promoting the product in global markets, generating profits and consequently destabilizing Chinese monopoly in tea trading. Like other transcontinental business of coffee, cocoa and sugar, tea became a success in England and America first. The government as well as private companies like Lipton and Brooke Bond were taken aback. Soon, what started as a colonial experiment became the pride of the colonized country, forever changing Bengali mornings.

In 1903, the Tea Promotion Board began active promotion of tea both in England and India; pertinently, the Indian Tea Association, a planter's agency, was already at it. 'In 1901, the Indian Tea Association woke up to the fact that their largest market was sitting right on their doorstep and extended their marketing campaign in the subcontinent. The Tea Association began by employing a superintendent and "two smart European travellers" to visit grocers. Their task was to persuade them to stock more tea on the shelves.'[57]

This was one of the marketing strategies to popularize tea, once an exclusive at chota hazris and tea parties hosted by the EIC officials styled on the lines of their counterpart in London. Deeply related to self-fashioning, tea became a means for showing off both for expat British population as well as for bhadraloks and the nouveau riche Bengalis.

As Lizzy Collingham notes:

> By the end of the eighteenth century, tea had become *the*
> British drink. At first a herbal remedy for the wealthy elite,
> it soon became a fashionable beverage. It provided a good
> replacement for the glass of sweet wine that aristocratic
> ladies used to take with a biscuit in the afternoons, and
> it allowed them to show off their collection of delicate
> porcelain tea bowls.[58]

Back in India, appropriating English lifestyle became a trend.
The local affluent redesigned their lives. In *Chelebelar Dinguli*,
Punyalata Chakraborty mentions how her family was frequent
hosts to get-togethers, where the European guests visiting their
home would rave about their dinnerware and serving ware.[59]
It would not be far-fetched to say that the city's Bengali elites
were aware of social mobility, which a fine life offered (read
Eurocentric) and drinking tea was a marker of this mobility.
'Costly tea sets, necessary arrangements for the serving of tea
and a habit of drinking tea with guests nicely fitted the bill
for the cultural aspirations of this class, eager to refashion
traditional sociability after western norms.'[60]

Fictional as it may seem now, many were dead against tea,
including Gandhi.[61] Calcutta had its local group of detractors
as well who were quite vocal and had good enough reasons
to oppose the brew. Most of their reasons centered around
oppressions of tea labourers at the plantations. 'In [the] 1880s,
at a time when the campaign to expose the oppression of
the plantation labourers was at its peak, Sundari Mohan Das
(1857–1950), the renowned doctor and Krishna Kumar Mitra
(1852–1936), the nationalist leader, gave up tea drinking for

good as a mark of protest.'[62]

Beyond labour repression, a dark reality, some had problematic rationale going against tea and the Bengali scientist and swadeshi entrepreneur Prafulla Chandra Ray was prime amongst them. His arguments were built around the cons of drinking tea, but once scientific reasoning failed, he sighted an additional justification that was enmeshed in patriarchal morality, 'that tea as a stimulant ultimately tended to impair one's brain and spoil one's appetite. It also made innocent housewives addicted and wayward, thus corrupting the pristine and pure domain of zenana (*suddha Antahpur*)—an anxiety clearly based on gender bias'.[63]

Yet, tea was unstoppable; its popularity rose through the events that followed. Demands of World War I meant more factories rolled out, railway networks expanded and industrial development hurriedly implemented. Greater Calcutta had several manufacturing units and jute mills. Millions got employed in these units and for them, tea—a low-cost, readily available drink—was an energy booster.

Collingham mentions:

> By 1919, the tea canteen was firmly established as 'an important element in industrial concern.' Thus, tea entered Indian life as an integral part of the modern industrial world that began to encroach on India in the twentieth century.
>
> The railways were another example of the arrival of the industrial world in India, and the Tea Association transformed them into vehicles for global capitalism.[64]

The tea stalls were located at strategic spots, closer to the platforms, for vendors were compelled to run along the side of the platform as the train chugged in.

Collingham further notes that, 'They equipped small contractors with kettles and cups and packets of tea and set them to work at the major railway junctions in the Punjab, the Northwest Frontier and Bengal. The cry of "*Chai! Gurram, gurram chai* (Tea! Hot, hot tea) mingled with the shouts of *pani* (water) carriers calling out "*Hindu pani*", "*Muslim pani*".'[65]

Thomas Lipton of Lipton Tea Company went all out to grab the tea market of Calcutta. Thomas had already done his groundwork successfully in England, impressing upon the average Britisher the Indianness of tea. He advertised Indian tea, and was able to sell at a much lower price than English grocers. 'By 1909, tea was associated to British minds with India to such an extent that it was worth Lipton's while to employ an Indian to stand in front of one of his London cafés as an advertisement.'[66] It was now Lipton's turn to capture the Bengali imagination. The idea was to come up with a masterstroke that would keep its prime competitors—Brooke Bond and Balmer Lawrie—at bay.

Lipton decided to innovate their packaging. Soon, the company came up with colourful packs of tea, which had illustrations drawn to titillate the memories of chota hazri, which was loved by the British. The strategy worked well, for bhadraloks, too, who could relate instantaneously to these advertisements. The sweet lure of appropriating an English breakfast—in a nutshell, a European way of life—was a sure-shot way to scale up in social mobility. Brooke Bond countered Lipton with its first-ever tea packed in vacuumed tins.

The popularity of tea remained unabated, even though popular culture retorted with banters, sometimes in favour of tea and sometimes against it. Gautam Bhadra, cultural historian, observes:

Dwijendralal Roy (1863–1913), the dramatist, songwriter and satirist, expressed in a humourous ode, his feeling that the regular supply of a single cup of morning tea was heavenly bliss. With the beverage, a piece of a toast and a morsel of egg were also welcome. A report of the early decades of the 20th century suggests that a cup of tea in the morning made one a perfect Bengali gentleman, while sipping twice a day turned him into a sahib. Ceaseless craving for this new beverage, however, would brand him as a *chinaman* (a man from China). 'Tea mindedness' among the urban Bengali enthusiasts during the 30s had acquired a new colloquial coinage chatal ('cha' or tea with 'tal' as a suffix), or tea addict, a word that has the obvious cultural resonance of *matal*, the Bengali word for a tippler.[67]

By the 1930s, nearly all junctions, stations, canteens and groceries had billboards with prominent signages that gave out loud and clear messages promoting the goodness of tea. Advertisements were carried out in vernacular newspapers by private brands as well as by the Indian Tea Promotion Board, the government's promoting agency, with categorical instructions on how to make a perfect cup of tea, as well as touting it as the nation's drink, accessible to one and all.

A quick and leisurely cup of tea was now a part of Bengali daily life. Popular dailies *Basumati, Jugantar, Anandabazar Patrika* and *Muhammadi* carried various types of adverts emphasizing tea as a happening thing. Some of these advertisements had a dainty housewife making tea, while others signed off with punchlines like 'Indian Tea: The World's Best Drink', 'India's Best Drink: Tea' and even something as righteous as 'Your Right, Your Glory: Tea', along with the artwork of a family enjoying tea.

Gautam Bhadra in *From an Imperial Product to a National Drink* notes that in the early 1930s, Subimal Roy, a nondescript schoolmaster, formulated a taxonomy of tea that would baffle any tea connoisseur. Roy categorized tea according to the mixture of ingredients used, the taste and the colour under a number of ingenious nomenclatures, such as *Baishnav bhogya cha*, which is tea suitable for a devotee of Vishnu, *Hanuman bhogya cha*, which is favourable for Lord Hanuman and *Janashadharan bhogya cha*, which is tea meant for commoners.[68]

This gripping and complex grouping of tea drinkers, conceived by Subimal Ray shows how tea had quickly become a part of everybody's life. Chatals or tea addicts were by no means fictitious.

Tea became a decisive element in Bengali social life. Its presence and consumption brought chatter and camaraderie, packed in the word 'adda', which would mean quintessential Bengali talkativeness, resulting in a romantic meet up or typical political debates over cups of tea.

Cafés dotting the city had a prominent suffix or byline in their signage: *chai-er cabin* (a tea café or a tea room). The tea rooms would soon become a prototype, serving a massy version of English breakfast, a fixed menu of tea with milk and sugar, bread toasts with butter or a dollop of jam (payable extra), a fluffy omelette fried in mustard oil, and one or two boiled eggs.

Chai-er cabin became the in thing, a hangout of sorts for educated young couples, men binging on political discussions and a downtime venue for women shoppers, unescorted. There was a sense of comfort to these places and Bengalis across gender found themselves at home in these addas. The tea room culture continued way into the 1970s, by when some of them had added private cubicles naming them 'special or ladies cabin' meant for couples or women's group, desirous of some uninterrupted chit-chat on their day out.

The most reputed names in literature headed by Rabindranath Tagore, Rajshekhar Basu (aka Parshuram), Sarat Chandra Chattopadhyay, Premankur Atorthy and Syed Mujtaba Ali were quick to induct situations around such tea meets in their stories and novels.

Once talkie cinema happened (in 1931), filmmakers, too, followed the footsteps of the novelists. Humorous situations around morning tea were a part of *Sharey Chuattar* (1953), the first of many super hits that Uttam Kumar and Suchitra Sen would deliver.

A romantic comedy, *Sharey Chuattar* is the story of a working men's lodge, where all residents wait their turn of morning tea served by a lone runner, invariably leading to comic situations. Later, tea sessions became customary in almost all early Uttam-Suchitra flicks.

On other instances, women drinking tea together would signal progressiveness. Aarti, the salesgirl in Satyajit Ray's *Mahanagar* (1963), is shown unhesitatingly enjoying a cup of tea with her female coworkers. She even ventures out on a tea cabin meet-up with her friend's husband to market her automatic knitting machines. These scenes symbolized Aarti's transition from a simple but intelligent housewife to a smart salesgirl, who had started negotiating the bad world, way beyond her own or her husband's expectation.

Calcutta got delightfully hooked onto tea and a typical round of tea would mean some little bites to go along. That was how the colloquial phrase *cha-er sathe ta* (a rhymed one, meaning tea with some bites) was born. This was the Bengali version of a tête-à-tête, or anytime tea and snacking, a gastro adventure; an acceptance of colonial modernity. Soon, snacking was considered both nutritive and a socially pleasurable act.

With tea and snacks inducted into the city's eating habits, it was a defining moment for amader khabar—an aspect of Bengali identity. Gautam Chakrabarti infers such induction as acts of hybridization,

> They were capable of hybridizing 'bileti' (<vilāyati=foreign, European) dishes to suit their epicurean—indeed even sybaritic—and/or eclectic tastes. This meant, to cite just one instance, that the mid-nineteenth-century English workers' staple 'fish and chips'—itself a hybrid, dating back to the sixteenth century, fashioned from the original Iberian pescados fritos by the Marranos and first made into a commercial success, in 1860, by a certain 'Joseph Malin, a Jewish immigrant newly arrived from Eastern Europe—became the 'fish-fry', which is one of Bengal's favourite heavy snacks.[69]

Fish fry, however, was not the lone snack to undergo Bengali domestication; in fact, it was just one of the many quick bites that Tapti Guha-Thakurta refers to as 'tapas like'[70]—a variety of chops, cutlets, fritters and fries.

In the 1940s, neighbourhoods saw the mushrooming of 'on-the-go snack points'. These snack points pushed the boundaries of hybridized food further to create a template of people's food.

Borrowing from British lunch and tiffin menu, they simplified the process of making a plate of chops, cutlets and fries. They were also not quite dependent on expensive fish, mutton or poultry; instead, they adapted to what was available at the local bazaars, mainly vegetables and kucho chingri (very small shrimps which are casually passed off in the grey zone of semi-vegetarian and non-vegetarian).

These snack points were typically called *telebhajar dokan* (shops dedicated to fries and fritters), which dished out delicious telebhajas made from potatoes, shrimp, eggs, brinjals, green bell peppers, spinach and banana flowers (mocha in Bengali).

The telebhajar dokans also required large quantities of batter, which was usually arrowroot or gram flour, combined with bread crumbs—both being crossovers from European list of ingredients. Snack points continue to be the common feature of the neighbourhood food scene of Kolkata even today, operating from late-afternoon hours, usually starting at four, which is the hour of *bikaler cha* (afternoon tea time).

The boundaries of what would be acceptable as amader khabar expanded. New definitions emerged from this culinary transformation. Hybridity, a sure sign of Bengali colonial modernity and fluid cosmopolitanism, was recognized, with simultaneous markers of 'pure' gastronomic identity being drawn. What survived in next few decades (by the 1970s) can be defined as *Kolkatar khabar* or Kolkata food—the delicious, emotion-evoking platter, which anyone connected to the metropolis would swear by, in the name of Kolkata; a cuisine that delivers the crux of Bangaliyana or the essence of being a Bengali.

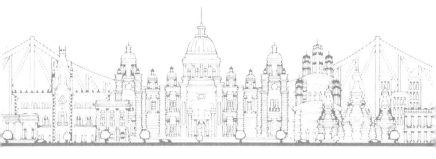

4

Tangerine Realities

Through the nineteenth century, Calcutta was at the centrality of British imperial interests. With urbanization and industrial development on the rise, factories were founded, railway networks began expanding, trade heightened, bazaars emerged and hundreds migrated to Calcutta from all over the country. The migrants were mostly working-class population for whom the city was their biggest reservoir of hope and livelihood. Utsa Ray writes: 'There were floating population of servants, cooks, gardeners, sweepers, washermen and similar groups among whom Bengalis and Odias figured most prominently.'[1]

When this section of the society moved into the city, their culinary culture, too, travelled with them, though it was limited to their community, distant from middle-class Bengalis. 'The bulk of the working population in Calcutta had no natural link with the respectable Bengali society in Calcutta.'[2] I will touch upon this observation a little later in the chapter.

Meanwhile, the great culinary mix-up was ongoing and its sources of pollination were more than one. Cookbooks remained the singular, most dominant channel of adaptability, along with the newly introduced curriculum at girls' schools and colleges. References affirm that cookery and kitchen-related education was an important component in the syllabi. 'With a view to avoid masculine training and meet the special requirements and develop the softer susceptibilities of the female mind, special subjects were included in the curriculum besides ordinary course of studies, such as domestic economy, drawing, music, cookery, needlework and laws of health,' observes Borthwick.[3] Emphasis was given on home management. 'Apart from their academic subjects, they learnt music, darning, sewing and knitting, and took turns at being kitchen monitor and keeping school accounts.'[4]

Once girls reached the tenth standard, they were trained in 'simple English cookery', which meant making tea, coffee, cocoa, mashed potato and potato chips as well as toasting bread. This continued to be a norm in Calcutta as recent as the 1980s. My personal experience of being introduced to cooking in senior school was channelled through the very same simple English cookery of tea and toasts. By then, it was interpreted as a 'simple Bengali breakfast', a colonial modernity that turned local.

At the turn of 1900, aspiring sugrihinis were the drivers of Bengali kitchens. They were encouraged to cook regularly for their husband and children. Cooking for one's loved ones was touted as a glorious, feminine act—a sacred mandate for women.

Despite cooking being projected as sacrosanct for women, when it came to bulk cooking, it was the men who took over. Male cooks from Odisha (erstwhile Orissa), locally addressed as *rannar thakur* (literally, the god of culinary; here, cook in-charge), were at the forefront of public cooking. They were a part of the population that had migrated to Calcutta in search of a livelihood.

Soon, they found a potential source of income by cooking in eateries that were exclusively meant for Hindu eaters. Such eateries often had signage like 'Hindu Bhojonalaya: The Hindu Eatery'.

Such eateries started emerging in large numbers towards the latter half of the nineteenth century and rannar thakurs, being Brahmins, were hired fast. For both owners of these eateries as well as for those who stepped in for a meal, the caste identity of the cooks mattered. It worked as a 'seal of purity', so to say, ensuring unadulterated food was cooked and served.

In contrast, Bengali Brahmin men hardly took up cooking as their livelihood. Instead, it was the prototype Bamun didi, a sisterly Brahmin widow often depicted in Bengali novels of the times, who would be hired as a cook with the large upper-caste families. That said, Odia rannar thakurs could enter into a kitchen of a 'respectable' Bengali household only under select circumstances.

The circumstances were multiple, like if the woman of the house was inept in cooking or the head of the family was liberal enough to hire outsiders, but most definitively, rannar thakurs were employed when the question of bulk cooking arose. This would be on weddings, engagement ceremonies and Durga Puja. Durga Puja celebrations held by certain families were exceptionally grand. From décor to food to the invitee list, each and every detail was meticulously taken care of and painstakingly planned, with abundant funds allocated, leading to this pompous affair. Food platters served were varied and depended on the guest category.

While the meal meant for charitable dispenses were vegetarian, there was another category—an eclectic, scrumptious line-up of drinks and eatables. The vegetarian fare was prepared only by rannar thakurs, while the fanciful, hybrid menu consisting of a mixed platter was attributed to more than one cook, both Hindus and Muslims, such as thakurs, and bawarchis and rakabdars, respectively. And then there was the Great Eastern Hotel, which was inundated with orders during Durga Puja meant for European invitees at the baboos' homes.

Two descriptions from the later decades of the nineteenth century enumerate social customs and the range of dishes cooked during these celebrations. Delicious desi food plate meant for large-scale public meal distribution would usually consist of 'different kinds of sweetmeats, fruits, *luchis*, vegetable curries &c,'[5] and sometimes khichri. The other non-desi menu reflects magnified indulgence—an exercise in luxury and self-fashioning, which the host took pride in.

Babu Shib Chunder Bose, an English-educated scribe, documenting his community in the last decades of the nineteenth century, observantly wrote:

> The room is furnished after the European fashion; chairs, tables, sofas, chiffoniers, cheval-glass, sideboard, pictures, glass and silver and plated-ware, knives, forks and spoons and I know not what more—all arranged in proper order, and friends of congenial taste had free access. First class wines and viands, such as Geisler's champagne, Heatly's port and sherry, Exshaw's brandy No. I, Crabbie's ginger-wine, Bass's best bottled beer, soda water, lemonade, ice, Huntley and Palmer's mixed biscuits, Manila cigars, cakes and fruits in heaps, *puláo, kurmá, kuptá, kálláya,* roast fowl, cutlets, mutton-chops, and fowl-curry are plentiful kept; and an English visitor is not an unwelcome guest. The Great Eastern Hotel Company should be thankful for the large orders with which the Hindoo aristocracy of Calcutta and its suburbs favour them during the grand festival.[6]

While that was impressions from Durga Puja, *paka dekhas* (engagement ceremonies) leading to weddings, were no less a lavish affair. This was the day to kick-start feasting; a typical lunch would consist of luchis and kachuris (both deep-fried flatbreads), vegetables curries, sweetmeats, fruits and other seasonal delicacies.

When stretched, it could be even more than 40 dishes, which close relatives of both the bride and the groom would relish. However, some would be sarcastic about this unnecessary show-off. In 1938, *Prabasi*, a well-known Bengali magazine, carried a write-up where the essayist banters his friend: 'Last year I was invited by my friend for his son's *paka dekha* and to my surprise it was much more than simple sweetmeats. There was *luchi, pulao*, meat and vegetable curries, chutney, sweetmeats, sweet curd, *rabri* and more. To my counting it would [be] more than forty dishes, if not more.'[7]

Interesting to note is how pulao or pilaf, an adapted rice dish, had secured a firm position for itself in Bengali cuisine. Pulao wasn't the only crossover. Kofta, quorma, kaliya/kalia (a thick fish gravy), cutlet, fry, chops, pudding and ice-cream, too, were prominent must-haves. While pulao, quorma, kofta, and their likes were by and large derivatives of Mughlai or Nawabi cuisine, the others like a fowl cutlet or a pudding were from the early Company days, reminiscent of chota hazri and burrah khana.

In another menu for an upwardly Bengali wedding of 1947, the list was long, with a total of nearly 138 items. These were divided into subcategories of luchi, pulao split into vegetarian and non-vegetarian varieties followed by plain rice, fish, meat, poultry dishes in the form of kofta and quorma, a variety of deep-fried snacks made of fish and vegetables addressed as bhajas, dals, pickles, chutneys, a plethora of rice puddings, fruits, sweetmeats, several kinds of sodas, digestives, and more.

In this list of more than a hundred dishes, there were several pulaos with intriguing names like Vishnu pulao or mutton croquette pulao. I would assume Vishnu pulao to be a rice dish in which no spices associated with the Nawabi platter are used and is perhaps cooked in milk. Croquette, on the other hand, was an indispensable element of burrah khana, the lavish dinner associated with the Company days in India. Croquette was frequently teamed up with rissoles, omelettes, and more. Made of fillings of cold meat and put in a binder, breaded and then deep fried in lard, croquettes was often considered an appetizer or hors d'oeuvres that most Europeans preferred before the main course was served. In the colonial life of Calcutta and other presidencies, croquette—a word originating in the French word 'croquer' meaning 'to crunch'—was fairly popular. Its acceptance in the British dining came in late, when Anglo-Indian cuisine was undergoing a shift and there was a tendency of serving French delicacies, thus minimizing quintessential Indian curries.

The menu also had innovations like cauliflower roast, cabbage Mirzapuri, alu jaihind, kumdor Hussain Shah and khirer mumlet. The vegetables used and the techniques are worth noting. While roasting is a method used in European cooking, usually associated with poultry and meat, when combined with cauliflower, it would certainly emerge as a doubly new concept—a new technique as well as a new vegetable used. To that, there were rising sentiments of nationalism, with names of dishes like alu jaihind and Vidyasagar barfi being considered patriotic.

The platter signals an explosion of hybridity, turning out to be the essence of Bengali cooking, where experimentations would sometimes border on eccentricity, like in the case of a khirer mumlet, or a sweet omlette. The word 'mumlet' is a colloquial distortion of the word 'omlette' by the Bengalis, as they got hooked on to eggs and, in this case, it would mean an omlette made of kheer or khoa (dried whole milk). Unusual as it may sound, these dishes were a reflection of heightened innovation, best trialed in a wedding menu.

All Bengali wedding meals ended in a massive serving of sweetmeats. They were special. I would consider them a feat accomplished by local confectioners known as moiras. No wedding meal worth their status would be complete without at least 20 varieties of them. A deep dive into the world of Bengali sweets therefore is inevitable and soon it would be.

The opulence of food during celebrations brings forth the need for speciality cooks, an idea that increasingly became acceptable to wealthy and elite Bengalis. Those who could hire all kinds of cooks: Hindu, Muslim and Christian males, who exclusively prepared their kind of good food—a genre in which they excelled, say, Mughlai or *bileiti khabar* (Bengali word for anything European; in this case, indicating mostly English and French cuisine).

The Tagores adopted newness and a hybrid lifestyle more readily than others. Thakurbari (the principal residence of the Tagore family at Jorasanko, Calcutta) had an atmosphere of openness, with many family members patronizing 'change'. Both daughters and daughters-in-law were permitted to attend schools. They were erudite, contributed to the growing cultural milieu, wrote, edited, painted, published journals and travelled abroad as well.

The poet laureate himself was a foodie, fond of mixed delicacies, particularly hilsa preparations, the choicest of kebabs and chingrir malai curry (prawn cooked in thick coconut milk). His wife, Mrinalini Devi, was a fine cook who 'used to make a range of sweetmeats and desserts. It was said that her delicious confections like *Mankaochur Jalipi* (Jaleibi made of Taro Corm), *Doier Malpoa* (Yogurt Pancake), *Paka Aamer Mithai* (Mango Dessert), *Chirer Puli* (Dumplings made of Flattened Rice) were unforgettable. Mrinalini inspired her husband to attempt cooking and in all likelihood he would goof up. Eventually it would be upon Mrinalini to salvage the situation'.[8]

The talented poet's wife was not the only one, there were other female members of the Tagore clan like novelist, poet and musician Swarnakumari Devi, Rabindranath's elder sister, and Gyanadanandini Devi, daughter-in-law of the Tagores and the wife of the first-ever IAS of Indian origin Satyendra Nath Tagore, Rabindranath's elder brother, who were raising the bar, and setting a precedence for others.

The men at home were supportive and it resonated in how they adapted to the new culinary tastes. Moreover, they were connoisseurs of good food. Thus, they left no stone unturned in stimulating their dining standards, hiring cooks from different backgrounds.

In a recollection of his younger days, playwright and musician Jyotirindranath Tagore (the fifth brother of Rabindranath Tagore), mentions a French cook named Cathrin at the Tagore household of Jorasanko: 'Cathrin was responsible for preparing the dinner for guests and the food for home was cooked by an upper caste hired cook. However, Cathrin also cooked for family members when they craved western food.'[9] Another reference details Abanindranath Tagore's (Rabindranath Tagore's nephew) delight around newly discovered food. Abanindranath, the founder of the Bengal School of Art, was a painter, littérateur and a foodie.

Utsa Ray explains:

But Tagore was not appreciative of such 'Bramhanical' dishes twice a day. Tagore in fact had an interesting take on such new culture of food. He told his grandsons that Taleb Ali's cooking could not compare anywhere near to the culinary skills of Navin, someone who cooked for the Tagores when he was young. However, Navin's forte was in cooking for gigantic parties, where tables where set in an elaborate manner with forks, spoons, knives arraigned (sic) in proper ways. But with time such culture had become much more domesticated. Hence Taleb Ali's cooking was perfect for a time when someone could cherish such new food within the comfortable zone of one's own house.[10]

Thus, there were the Taleb Alis, Navins and Catherins of the world (read bawarchis, rannar thakurs and French chefs) all in a single household. The Tagores were truly an emancipated lot, as employing a French female cook was not a norm in those days. However, what was becoming more of a noticeable pattern was the rising adaptability, an inclusiveness, which the upper middle-class Hindu Bengalis were willingly accepting. But there was a caveat to it. In an attempt to embrace new food, Bengalis were also seeking a distinct identity, which would help retain their existing food habits, packaged in what they imagined or understood as *Bangali khabar* (Bengali food) alias amader khabar. Sometimes, this would mean appropriating dishes only the way they wanted to. They were hooked on to eggs, and omelettes were usual in breakfasts; yet, they carefully excluded the cheese and mushroom variants. Similarly, when it came to consuming bread, their choice was basic butter or jam toast and not a sandwich. While cherishing a celebratory meal, pulao was more than welcome, but goshtt (meat) pulao was a big no. So, they chose what suited them most both caste and religion wise.

Little tweaks like ghee, an acceptable cooking medium, was used in chicken stew instead of a dollop of butter, which was still 'foreign' for some. When it came to appropriating spices, the women favoured mildly aromatic green cardamom as opposed to its strongly scented close cousin, the black ones, for rice pudding and pulaos.

In this climate of change and adaptations, male cooks played a crucial role, as mentioned earlier. There were religious restrictions in food meant for Hindu Bengali widows. Often, the rannar thakurs would come up with vegetarian alternatives to the very same dishes that normally would have an animal protein as its key ingredient. Such dishes served as substitutes for the fish quorma, kalia and dolma with mincemeat stuffing and, for that matter, any fish- or meat-based dish.

Some examples of these vegetarian innovations would be delicately cooked mochar ghanto (plantain flower blossom gravy), an alternative to mutton dishes and, moong dal with roasted diced coconut. The diced coconut would substitute the usual staple of fish head. There were several other vegetarian recipes which were equally elaborate and scrumptious, contrary to the popular conception about Bengali food. They reflect the culinary innovations by the rannar thakurs, and their Muslim brethren—the rakabdars and bawarchis, who were also credited with introducing the present-day indispensables of the Bengali platter often consisting of shukto (a bittersweet mixed vegetable sometimes cooked in a milk base), Bangali pulao (a sweeter variant of the pulao tailor-made for Bengali taste), kosha mangsho (rich gravy-based dish of goat or lamb meat), rui kalia (an adaptation of the kalia with the fatty, chunkier pieces of carp or katla) and mutton quorma.

Over time, these delicacies held the essence of amader khabar, not to forget that earlier they all had to be cleverly introduced to the community via weddings, engagement ceremonies and Durga Puja celebrations—a complex, time-taking process of appropriation and integration. It had also taken ample time for the educated elite and middle class to recognize the culinary knowledge of these unlettered working-class men: the rannar thakurs, bawarchis and the traditional moiras.

THE SWEET MAFIA ATTACK

There is no doubt that Bengalis have a fetish for sweets and it is Calcutta that became the epicentre of this obsession in the mid-nineteenth century. Though en masse addiction to sweetmeats is a relatively recent trend, its roots lay in antiquity of social history of the province, in which milk was a revered ingredient. Before rewinding, it must be mentioned that in the sweeping dominance of British and Mughal (loosely Muslim) food, the Portuguese stood their ground in colonial gastronomic narrative with their most important contribution of chhana or casein, a key ingredient in sweetmeats. But some deep diving in the 'milky way' first.

A brief entry of pāyasa(m), also spelt pāyesh, in K.T. Acharya's *A Historical Dictionary of Indian Food* reads, 'A sweetened dish of rice cooked in milk the *payasa* first finds mention in Buddhist Jain canonical literature in c.400 BC. Since common ingredients are used, the dish could well be very much older. It seems unchanged to this day, being called pāyasam in South India and pāyesh in Bengal.'[11]

Payesh is the most rudimentary form of sweet dish that the ancestors of colonial Bengalis have prepared and served. References of payesh, also called paramanna, literally meaning the 'best staple', goes back to Bengal's cultural history. Paramanna is considered pure food—a naivadya or offertory to the gods, as well as the first morsel of rice served to a Bengali Hindu baby. Pertinently, the importance of milk and rice cooked together and individually, too, are phenomenal and dates much earlier in history.

Paramanna finds mention in the narrative novellas of the medieval period. Written in poetry format, these novellas refer to the diets of the trinity of Hinduism, directly attributing to their temperament. The sixteenth-century *Chandi Mangal Kabya* (eulogy literature of Goddess Chandi), written by Kabikankan Mukandaram Chakraborty, describes Shiva's and Vishnu's dietary patterns. 'Shiva, who is considered choleric and prone to violence, eats food cooked with pungent mustard oil and not ghee. Vishnu on the other hand is imagined as having a serene temperament and is offered *sattivika* foods including tender vegetables cooked in ghee, and a variety of desserts, all derived from milk.'[12]

I am not agreeable on Shiva's disconnect to milk. Many Shaivite literatures depict Shiva as milk-reliant, a necessary supplement to his cannabis intake. Either way, references to milk were frequent in literature. In reality, milk and milk-based products were common in medieval Bengali diet. Moreover, paramanna 'was not only served to Gods but also was a human favourite. It was a featured food in most festive meals and many secular rituals.'[13] There is a much quoted Bengali saying that plays on the importance of rice pudding, a verse from Bharatchandra Ray Gunakarer's *Annada Managalkabya* (1752) (eulogy to the Hindu goddess of food and nourishment, Goddess Annada, an incarnation of Shiva's wife Parvati). The saying goes: *'Amar santan jeno thake dudhe bhāte'* (May my child be always blessed with the nourishment of rice pudding). With a poetic novella based on the power of the goddess of food, it is not far-fetched that a couplet, a metaphor for prosperity and well-being was conceived by its writer.

Beyond rice pudding, a variety of sweetmeats had been cited in a prime devotional biography of Chaitanya Mahaprabhu, a reformist mystic leader, titled *Chaitanya Charitamrita* (written by Krishnadasa Kabiraj in 1555). Chaitanya, formerly Nemai, who was born in an orthodox Brahmin family, later broke away from Brahmanical Hinduism, revolting against the discriminatory caste system. Like Gautam Buddha, he, too, left home, followed by thousands of oppressed, discriminated lower-caste denizens of Bengal. The biography enumerated on the life and times of the reformist, how he preached love, equality and brotherhood leading finally to the emergence of Vaishnavism in Bengal. However, his doctrine of non-violence came along with the concept of vegetarianism, somewhat unfamiliar to his disciples and Bengalis at large. Thousands were influenced by Chaitanya Mahaprabhu, like Rassundari Devi, who confessed in her book *Amar Jibon* how *Chaitanya Charitamrita* always healed her as a young wife and mother.

It is this milieu of a non-violent life that the early sweet-making culture of Bengal got its boost from.

In *Hour of the Goddess*, food historian Chitrita Banerji acknowledges Chaitanya Mahaprabhu's affinity for sweets:

A staggering variety of sweets are mentioned, indicating that despite his abjuration of human intimacy and worldly possessions, Chaitanya had a Bengali predilection of sweets. Many of these were made with puffed, popped or flaked rice, combined with white or brown sugar and/or kheer. Others were concocted from flour, coconut, grounded legumes, or sesame seeds. Krishnadas also mentions an impressive array of purely milk based sweets—kheer mixed with slice mangoes, sweet yogurts and items like *dughdha-laklaki, sarbhaja, sarpupee and sandesh*.[14]

In their present-day avatar, dughdha-laklaki is the much-loved rabdi and sarpupee is sarpuria (sweets made of popped, puffed or flattened rice combined with white or brown sugar; synonymous with Krishnanagar of the Nadia district in present-day West Bengal, where the spiritual leader was born). Not only the *Mangal Kabyos*, other sixteenth-century texts, too, mention a wide arc of sweets, such as chhanabora, khaja, jilebi, modak, malpua, sita misri and sandesh, emphasizing Bengali's affinity for sweets and sweetened dishes. References of these sweets would resurface again in popular memory and also in cookbooks after three centuries as Bengal would embark on its most fructive period of artisanal sweet-making.

Unlike the chhana-based sweetmeats, which are very popular today, the cited ones were made of either sar or khoa kheer. Sar (differently spelt as 'shar') is the cream that forms the top layer of the milk when boiled for hours. This would then be skimmed to make sweets with the binding of sugar, molasses and grated coconut. The other key ingredient used to make sweets those days was kheer. Though 'kheer' is the quintessential Hindi word for rice pudding, the word originated in the Sanskrit word 'ksheer', which is a derivative of thickened milk. Kheer can be either gooey or a soft grainy milk compound, also called khoa kheer, which has the virtue of remaining unspoiled than any other form of milk, an important consideration in a humid, tropical climate.

Krishnanagar had developed a unique skill in handling dairy variants like sar and khoa kheer. Till today, fond memories of Krishnanagar-er kheerer putul, or figurines made of khoa kheer, peppers conversations centred around sweetmeats. Informal chatters refer to crowded stalls of sweetmeats from Krishnanagar, with kids eyeing trays of delectable sweets through those grainy glass chests. The chests would mostly contain an array of dolls, resembling a Bengali family, all made of kheer and sometimes, a bouquet of juicy fruits with mangoes, peaches, custard apples and bananas. It is fascinating, how the new fruits found their place as sweetmeats along with the fruits traditionally available in Bengal.

The joy of savouring kheer-er mishti (sweets made of kheer) was pure as was its medium.

Fast forward from days of *Chaitanya* to the late sixteenth-century Bengal, when the Portuguese, whose story would be overshadowed by the English, came to India. It is worth nothing that their brief connect with Bengal had been remarkable. Known for their 'enterprise and consummate bravery', the Portuguese rose to commendable heights as a trading entity during the rule of the Mughal emperor Akbar, who granted them permissions to trade. By 1599, they had built a settlement on the Hooghly with a church and fortress to themselves.[15]

The emergent cultural tapestry around the river became diverse and colourful. The Portuguese were the first to park, along with the Dutch, Danes, Armenians and finally the British, all settling close to the river. Each community led a unique life, recreating their 'homelands' as much as Bengal's weather and topography would permit them. It is here in Bandel, a word derived from the Bengali word 'bondar', meaning port that the culture of cheese making began. The Portuguese settlers were prosperous. They traded in salt, tobacco, cotton, gunpowder and more, across all of Indies and Europe. The wealthier lot led an elaborate life reliving the ways of Portugal. Women were skilled in processing milk and soon renewed the making of *queijo fresco,* which literally means 'fresh cheese' in Portuguese.

Observers, over the years, had drawn similarities between queijo fresco and York cream cheese, feta cheese of Greece and even ricotta of Italy, but in the reality, traditional fresh cheese of Portugal is distinct in its form. It is a white, lightly textured, mildly salty and unripened cheese, made of goat, buffalo or cow milk originating from the Iberian Peninsula area of Portugal, at best a close cousin of the others. Consumed fresh in its country of origin over a toasty warm bread or just like that along with a cup of espresso, this variety of cheese in its smoky variant acquired a local name 'Bandel cheese'. They came in cake form: small, chunky, slightly flattened like a disc, not more than one-and-a-half-inch in diameter.

What seemed habitual to Portuguese women of Hooghly and its neighbourhood guided the reimagining of sweetmeat-making, revolutionizing Bengali gastronomic narrative forever. Henceforth, it would be the triumphant journey of chhana, broadly referred to as cottage cheese. While the cheese they innovated, both Bandel cheese and Dhakai paneer (then available only in Dhaka), had been mostly forgotten, it was their unique milk-processing techniques that were still remembered. On those very lines, the Portuguese contributed to Bengali sweetmeat-making.

Buddhadeb Bose, a noted Bengali author of the mid-twentieth century, was fairly excited at the uniqueness of chhana as medium, 'I do not know of any other part of India or the world where milk is turned to casein—the Bengali word is "chhana", and I'm not sure if the English expression is quite accurate. Chhana is the base of all the famous creations of the Bengali confectioner. Its nearest Occidental equivalent is cottage cheese.'[16]

While Acharya, in his food dictionary, simply puts it, 'The precipitation of milk with slightly acid whey or rather acidulants yields solids in the form of chhāna; this is especially in Bengal the basis of innumerable sweetmeats.'[17]

Classified under 'acid curd cheese', chhana ushered in a new era. Historical evidences of curdling of milk are mentioned by Acharya in his book *Indian Food: A Historical Companion*: 'Whey was prepared by adding acid fruit juices to boiled milk to precipitate the solids which were then strained away.'[18] The only elements used for curdling milk were naturally acidic as milk was considered sacred.

Probing deep into the etymology, Banerji notes,

> The etymology of the term is rather obscure, but according to several major Bengali dictionaries, it is case of a verb becoming a noun. Chhana is related to another verb *shana*, both meaning kneading rigorously by hand to create a fine paste or dough. The naming of chhana seems based on the fact that all chhana based sweets require the curdled milk solid to be first kneaded.[19]

However, 'chhana' does not find any mention till as late as the mid-seventeenth century, until it was introduced by the Portuguese via lactic acid extracted from whey. Inherently crumbly, with a mild binding element, it surely needed some kneading. And it is here that Nobin Chandra Das's brilliant, curious story comes to play. While the world celebrates his achievement of being able to transform casein into a perfect spherical ball dipped in sugar syrup, Das's story is also a tale of determination, of reclaiming the identity of the quintessential moiras of Bengal.

Nobin's family was sugar merchants from Burdwan, who later moved to Calcutta. With their family business dwindling, he was compelled to take up a job with a distant relative who had a sweet shop at Baghbazaar, north Calcutta. Determined, Nobin decided to take life head-on. Soon, he started his own sweet shop in the Jorasanko area, where he diligently tried experimenting with chhana and how to bind it. Though the quality of chhana that Nobin produced was superior to others, while boiling it in sugar syrup, it would either disintegrate or get burnt. Despite failed attempts to bind chhana, Nobin did not give up, and finally in 1868, through reverse osmosis, the 22-year-old confectioner successfully came up with a tight round ball. Nobin noticed for the first time how the ball didn't fall apart when dipped in sugar syrup. Hardly knowing what destiny had in store, he named his discovery as literal as it could get: roshogolla ('rosh' in Bengali means 'syrup' and 'golla' refers to anything round). Rest, as they say, is history!

Whether roshogolla belongs to Bengal or Odisha can be a matter of argument, but it is surely Nobin Moira, aka Nobin Chandra Das, who had made roshogolla a sweetmeat that one knows today, wondrously legendary as its western counterpart, chocolates.

With the roshogolla's discovery, hundreds of moiras understood the longevity of chhana and that it can attain a better shelf life when prepared Nobin's way. Consumers, too, became totally enamoured by the pristine round mass, its soft, spongy melting effect in the mouth. An expansive playbook of chhana was emerging.

The next-big sweet invention would be the sandesh and together with roshogolla, it would sweep Bengalis off their feet. Sandesh had been referred to in the medieval texts but not the types that survive today. What was offered to the deities or to the religious leaders like Chaitanya were made of khoa kheer. Once chhana was invented, the kanchagolla, the most humble form of sandesh, came into being. Moulded by hand with light pressure, it is sweetened chhana.

'Golla' is of course anything round, but how did the word 'kancha' get added? Literally, 'kaccha' means 'imperfectly cooked' and pucca, its opposite, but ritual usage goes beyond this. Kaccha foods are basically foods cooked in water.[20]

Extending this definition, the kanchagolla—the first and most basic sandesh—is a derivative of milk, with segregation of whey (liquid) and solid, thus ritualistically considered as kaccha. Perhaps this is the reason that the simplest of sandesh is considered the most unadulterated form of chhana by Bengalis and can be served even to the ailing. 'Soon Sandesh began to be cast in various molds (to resemble flowers, fruit and shells), given various colours sweetened with palm jaggery, sugarcane, jaggery, and sugar coated to yield manōhari and flavoured with jackfruit, orange peel and rose essence,' writes Acharya in *A Historical Dictionary of Indian Food*.[21]

The Portuguese traveller and monk Fray Sebastien Manrique, travelling from Bengal to Punjab in the 1630s, noted that the Bengalis had 'many kinds of lecteus [lacteous] food and of sweetmeats prepared in their own way for they have great abundance of sugar in those parts'.[22] The good Manrique may well have succumbed to temptation for he reports, 'Entire streets could be seen wholly occupied by skilled sweetmeat makers, who proved their skill by offering wonderful sweet scented daunties (sic) of all kinds which would stimulate the most jaded appetite to gluttony.'[23]

Riding on this legacy emerged today's heritage confectioners—the sandesh specialists Bhim Chandra Nag, Girish Chandra Dey and Nakur Chandra Nandy, K.C. Das (Nobin Chandra Das's family brand), Nabakrishna Guin, Sen Mahasay and Putiram, all starting out in the decades of the nineteenth century, a time when Calcutta was gloriously cosmopolitan with ample opportunities for innovators.

Thrilling things happened in the world of sweetmeats in the next years.

Soon, Krishna Chandra Das, popular in present times as K.C. Das, set up his manufacturing unit K.C. Das and Co. He had by then invented the second-most memorable sweetmeat from his stable—the delicate rasmalai, which resembled patties made of chhana and was soaked in sweetened milk.

Many products were developed by enterprising moiras: kheer mohan and cham-cham, mouchak (shaped like a beehive), sitabhog resembling rice grains, gulab-jamun, lal-mohan, totapuri, etc. Pantua and chitrakoot are again chhana based and in Bengal even jilebi is termed as chhanar jilipi and employs chhana to create whorls that are deep fried before placing in syrup.[24]

Started by Param Chandra Nag in 1826 and inherited by his son Bhim Chandra Nag, the present-day sandesh of Kolkata is synonymous with this confectioner. Soon, the sandesh, simple in its form and look, took birth at their Bowbazaar Street shop.

Unassumingly called 'makha sandesh' (mashed, hand-pounded), it was an accidental creation, a well-meaning thought to prevent the wastage of chhana. With no refrigeration and soaring temperatures, particularly in summer, a large volume of chhana had to be discarded by the end of the day. The innovative confectioner came up with the idea of adding ground cardamom, sugar and khoa to increase its shelf life. The final shapes could be anything: simple rounds like kanchagolla or disc shaped.

After that, there was no looking back. Perhaps, it was a divine interplay between the celestial and human agencies that Bengali sweets rolled on its golden journey. In consolidating its massive outreach, patrons like Rani Rashmoni, a Hindu woman zamindar from the Jan Bazaar area and a philanthropist of her times, played a major role. Rashmoni founded a Kali temple at Dakhineshwar, on the eastern bank of the Hooghly, in 1855. She ordered 28 maunds[25] of sandesh on the day the temple was inaugurated. Her chief priest, popular religious leader Ramakrishna Paramahamsa, better known as Vivekananda's spiritual mentor, was another important connoisseur of the sandesh.

In love with what food historian Michael Krondl describes as a 'haiku' of sweets aka the sandesh, Ramakrishna had standing instruction for his closest disciples to fetch the delicacy whenever they would visit him. In fact, Nobin Chandra Das's dedo sandesh was dedicated to Sri Sharada, the wife of Ramakrishna.

The Bengali intelligentsia, too, wholeheartedly supported enterprising confectioners. Tagore was fond of Nobin Moira's roshogolla, so was Ashutosh Mukherjee, the vice chancellor of Calcutta University. Mukherjee gorged on Bhim Nag's abar khabo. The pioneer confectioner created a special sandesh named Ashu-bhog, dedicating it to his doting patron. The legend goes that Ashutosh's buggy would stop at Bhim Nag's every morning on its way to Calcutta University and Bhim Nag himself would keep his daily parcel of sweetmeats ready.

Countless stories of excellence in sweet-making and their subsequent appreciation have permeated the palimpsest of the city's history but none beats the top stories; the clock with Bengali numerical and of abar khabo, ledikeni.

Abar khabo is a delectable indulgent sandesh that Nobin Chandra Das created especially for Maharani Swarnamoyee Devi of Cossimbazar, who apparently had got bored of the existing repertoire of sweetmeats. Ledikeni (the alternate spelling of Lady Canning), on the other hand, was a dedication to the vicereine, the wife of Viceroy and Governor General Charles Canning. Conceived by Bhim Nag, ledikeni—an oblong, golden-brown, deep-fried sweetmeat stuffed with raisins and cardamom powder—is a variant of the Bengali pantua (deep-fried balls of semolina, chhana and sugar syrup). Shrouded with fascinating versions of stories, ledikeni is remembered by almost all in Calcutta. The more popular anecdote has Charles Canning wanting to gift his wife a special dessert on her birthday and asked the prominent confectioner to make one exclusively for the occasion, leading to the birth of ledikeni, the sweet.

The other trivia is how a motley group of confectioners from Behrampore, Murshidabad created the sweetmeat to commemorate Lady Canning's visit to India in 1858. Whatever is the more authentic version of the anecdote, the first lady loved the confection. After her demise, the popularity of the sweet grew remarkably. With the passage of time, the sweetmeat came to be known as ledikeni (a pronunciation abrasion of Lady Canning, by which it is known till date).

In 1858, Robert Thomas Cooke of Cooke and Kelvey (C&K), British India's most sought-after silverware and timepiece maker, known for their finest Swiss movements, happened to visit Bhim Nag's Bowbazaar shop. Delighted by the sweet allure of Nag's creations, Cooke wanted to gift Nag a clock, which was surprisingly missing in his outlet. Nag then requested for Bengali numerical on the clock, so that his karigars (workers) could sense time. Cooke obliged, and till date, the heritage timepiece adorns the wall of Bhim Nag's Bowbazaar outlet.

Artisanal sweetmeats were being created, and confectioners were coming up with innovations. Some even decided to name their creations on colonial governors and their first ladies. For example, the ledikeni that was named after Lady Canning. A sandesh was named after Lord Ripon, Viceroy from 1880 to 1884. In the 1960s, a sandesh was called bulganiner bishmoy (Bulganin's wonder) honouring the Soviet premier Nikolai Bulganin's visit. Perhaps such naming were conscious acts, strategies to find their place within the closed-door elite society of Calcutta.

Eventually, entrepreneurial grit of this nature compelled a shift in the social positioning of a moira, resulting in a move up in their social ladder. To that, they sometimes unknowingly mentored women who didn't belong to their caste or social status earning themselves the epithet of a 'guru'. Saradsundari Debi, the mother of the famous Brahmo reformist Keshab Chandra Sen, in her memoir *Phire Dekha* (Looking Back) describes how she and her widowed sister-in-law learnt cooking from a confectioner, with their domestic help acting as a messenger bringing back the tips that the confectioner offered.[26] Such incidents only heightened the reputation of the moiras. Yet, there were others who were unwilling to see a point in their growing popularity. Ironically, every celebration had the undeniable presence of sweetmeats of both kinds: home-made as well as the ones made by the confectioners.

Babu Shib Chunder Bose, who wrote an anthropological, well-observed treatise of the community titled *Hindoos As They Are* included various customs and festivities with a detailed account of the food cooked, served and consumed. 'The very best kinds of *loochees*, *kocharees*, vegetable curries, fruits, sweetmeats and other delicacies of the season are to be provided for this special occasion (referring to a marriage platter). *Loochee*, *Sundesh mittoye*, *burfi*, *rasagullah*, *sittavog*, &c., the ordinary food of the Hindoos on festive days, are at a discount.'[27]

When it came to Lady Canning, the sweetmeat, Bose made a bittersweet remark,

> The Bengalis have become so much anglicized of late that they have not hesitated to give an English name to their sweetmeats. When the late Lord Canning was the Governor General of India, it was said his Baboo made a present of some native sweetmeats to Lady Canning, who was kindly pleased to accept it. Hence the sweetmeat is called 'Lady Canning,' and to this day no grand feast among the Bengalis is considered as complete unless the 'Lady Canning' sort is offered to the guests. The man that first made it is said to have gained much money by its sale. It is not the savoury taste of the thing that makes it so popular, but the name of the illustrious Lady.[28]

Bose criticized the confectioner dismissing such naming as an overwhelming colonial burden on Bengalis. He further comments on the rising price of chhana tagging it as the 'most expensive product'.

He says:

> From 32 Rupees a maund (82 lbs), the normal price of *sundesh* in ordinary times, it rises to 60 or 70 Rupees in the Poojah time. Milk sells at four annas a pound, and without milk no *sundesh* could be made. It is the most expensive article of food among the Hindoos of Bengal, when well made with fresh *channa* (curdled milk) it has a fine taste, but is entirely destitute of nutritive property.[29]

The business of sweetmeat-making was evidently growing, faster than what even the insiders had envisaged. A profit out of chhana meant much incentive for the moira to work on his innovations. Girish and Nakur situated themselves in this space, a father-in-law and son-in-law duo whose artisanally created sandesh was a class apart. Krondl enumerates an anecdote around the unbound love for Girish and Nakur's sandesh:

> When Ravi Shankar, the Bengali-born sitar virtuoso, returned to Kolkata in December 2007 after an absence of seven years, he was met by a mob of VIPs, TV reporters and cameramen. Yet, he did not immediately address the media huddle. He turned instead to a group of friends with a question that made some people wonder at the real reason for his trip. 'Tell me,' he whispered, 'is it that Nakur still makes that *sandesh*?' Of course, everyone gathered there knew what he meant. In Kolkata, Nakur is the prince of confectioners, renowned for his *sandesh*, a delicate sweet that every Kolkatan claims as his birthright.[30]

Neither was Ravi Shankar just being plain nostalgic, nor Krondl, who addresses Nakur Chandra Dey as the 'prince of confectioners' too off the mark. Sandesh definitely is the birthright of anyone from Calcutta. It is perhaps one of the most exclusive of all the intangible heritage that the city ever had! That said, if one manages to reach 56, Ramdulal Sarkar Street in a gloaming hour, evading the annoying traffic of north Calcutta to their final destination—the original shop of Girish Chandra Dey and Nakur Chandra Nandy, then certainly there is a conviction that is associated to this trip and Ravi Shankar's remark reflects that belief system.

It breathes of a Bengali's immense reliance on what Nakur delivers—the sheer poetry of sweetness. But no kingdom of any kind is built overnight—neither of gastronomic beliefs nor of the actual confection. Of the many confectioners who changed the sweetmeat scene of Calcutta in the nineteenth century, transforming sweetmeat to an identity were the father-in-law and son-in-law duo who began their humble shop in north Calcutta's Hedua, near Bethune College, in 1844. Nakur hailed from a confectioner family of Janai in Hooghly and was married into this Calcutta-based family of confectioners. Soon, they started a joint venture. He was gifted and innovative, owing to his Hooghly DNA, a province that had been linked to sweetmeat-making earlier than Calcutta. After all, the Portuguese were based in Hooghly.

Even today, a hole-in-the-wall shop, the methods of making sandesh is meditatively simple and delightfully manual. With a handful of huge karahis and deghs (cauldrons), only cow milk is pasteurized by boiling and creamy chhana is indulgently extracted and kneaded manually. Every day, the prince of confection churns out a quota of their original repertoire:

natungurer kadapak (a harder version of the sandesh with a longer shelf life), jalbhora talsans (palmyra-shaped sandesh with a centre-fill), dilkhush (which means 'my joyous heart'), monohara (another variant of the sandesh meaning 'the one who allures me') and golapkhas (a fragrant rose-scented sandesh).

Then, there is kadapak, an art as they say and this is what the heritage confectioner is most famed for. Resembling a palmyra fruit, the chunky sweetmeat, a much-loved winter delectable of Bengal, is made of chhana and fresh palm jaggery. To obtain that melt-in-the-mouth effect, it is cooked in a consistency that's unique to this traditional confectioner. The other much-admired sandesh from their stable is natungurer jalbhora (a sandesh with a centre-fill of palm jaggery). However, 'jalbhora' is a generic term for any centre-fill and this could be a rose syrup, caramel filling, liquid chocolate, and more.

Jalbhora is immensely popular even today as it was in 1881, when a confectioner based in Chandannagore (a French settlement in the Hooghly district) came up with 'an oasis by pouring rose syrup inside the sandesh'. The architect of this sweet oasis was Surya Kumar Modak (Modak indicates the confectioner's caste). More stories around the popularity of the jalbhora have got added to the food lore over the years, one of them being about a Frenchman from Chandannagore smitten by the sweetmeat.

These anecdotes underline how sweetmeats made of chhana were gradually integrated into the food choices of Bengal in the nineteenth century, though sweets were always there. Their acceptance into the everyday and celebratory food fare pushed boundaries. Moiras were able to make inroads into more literate and exclusive sections of the society. On a visit to some such age-old confectioners, one may come across photographs of their founders framed on the walls. The sepia-toned portraits look rather stylish with the posers in their layered dhoti-kurta and heavily embroidered Kashmiri shawls propped up with decorative flower vases on their sides. The portraits hardly resemble the conventional description of a Bengali confectioner in baniyan and dhotis, and instead pointed to their steadily rising social mobility.

By the early twentieth century, sweetmeats had formed a mini world of its own, within the larger canvas of Bengali cuisine. Bipradas Mukhopadhyay's *Mistanna Pak* (1906) made sweetmeat-making a serious affair for any Bengali woman willing to try it at home. Driven by the same intent as his earlier books *Pakrajeshwar, Byanjon Ratnakar* and *Pak Pranali* of 'reviving the art of cooking', this omnibus of dessert recipes and sweetmeats had an additional agenda of furthering the popularity of Bengali sweet dishes.

Through the 13 chapters, Mukhopadhyay takes his readers on a sweet trail, first with the mediums of making sweets, beginning with milk and its direct derivatives, such as khoa kheer and chhana, followed by the basic sweeteners like sugar and jaggery, specifying their qualities and varieties. By the end of the first three chapters, he already shares recipes of medieval-era sweets, many of which were made of unrefined sugar or jaggery like batasha, kodma, murki, chirar chakti, chinar murki, rabdi and dadhi (curd), along with a unique preparation called bajra makkan, which definitely is a close relative of what we now know as Greek yogurt. It is at the beginning of the third chapter, while introducing ghee and flour-based savouries like luchi-puri and kachoris that the author's take on commercial confectionary is truly revealed.

As an author of a food book who happened to be a

Brahmin, Mukhopadhyay is critical of the lower-caste moiras and their ways of preparing sweetmeats in bulk. He emphasized on home-based sweetmeats and cakes as healthier substitutes concluding the section with a snarky remark about the lack of hygiene at a quintessential sweetmeat outlet of those days! Interestingly, his style of writing had remained the same and in *Mistanna Pak*, like in his earlier works, footnotes detail the Ayurvedic interpretations of ingredients like milk, ghee, jaggery and flour, among others.

Ironically inclusive as always, he also acknowledges polyglot elements of Calcutta with the distinct presence of Marwari sweets like ghewar, Nawabi (or loosely Mughlai) sweet delicacies including sweetened breads like bakharkhani and sheermal and desserts like golapi firni, semui and seyyaii (the present-day sewaiiya). Mukhopadhyay also lists the recipes of common European desserts like Christmas cake, Queen's cake, Madeira cake, sponge cake and the Portuguese bebinca or bebinka, to name just a few.

Flipping through the pages of *Mistanna Pak,* one finds recipes for milk loaf, apricot and tutti-fruity bread, singara (samosa), nimki (now part of the generic namkeen, earlier considered a light snack not more than half inch in size and mostly home-made), cakes made of orange peels and dry fruit, puddings, murabbas, baklava, vermicelli (seyyaii) and fruit-based custards.

However, the star draw of the book is not only the myriad recipes but also an emphatic list of 49 most popular and must-have Bengali sweetmeats beginning with golla sandesh, which would mean kanchagolla and included roshogolla, cham-cham, manoranjan, abar khabo, khirpuli, ata sandesh, Lord Ripon, Lady Canning, golapi peda, good morning, Nayantara, talsans, jalbhora talsans, khir mohan, chhana bhaja, kheerer sandesh, monad, dedo monda, various fruit replicas made of khoa kheer, rashamundi, alhade putul (the ecstatic doll, a figurine made of khoa kheer), golap jam (would corrupt to gulab jamun later), and more.

Interpreting what survived over the decades and then disappeared, too, would reveal the deep connect that Bengalis have developed with their sweetmeats, who by then were in the habit of savouring mishti at any hour of the day. How important sweetmeats were for the locals can be gauged from the dizzying list of sweet dishes served at one of the elite weddings way back in 1947. The menu card read 38 varieties including both sandesh and syrupy sweets, excluding a dozen of murabbas and half-a-dozen of payesh or rice pudding!

In the next few decades, almost every lane of Calcutta had their much-loved shops. These confectionaries were mostly peer-reviewed, happy, proud markers of the mohallah. While the famous ones like K.C. Das, Girish Chandra Dey and Nakur Chandra Nandy, Bhim Nag, and their likes were special visits to celebrate the significant events of life, it was the local hole-in-the-wall confectioner that became the everyday go-to sweetmeat hub for many.

Chhanar mishti (sweetmeats made of chhana) made by the moiras was soon an undeniable imprint in the map of Calcutta's food, integrated into the fold of amader khabar. Irrefutably, its popularity had connections with Calcutta's colonial modernity, which induced the ability to open up when it came to any food prepared outside home.

Thereafter, mishti was omnipresent in Bengali cinema, novels, essays and even syndicated comics. In this abundant celebration of delectable sweet edibles, nothing beats the grandiose climax of Satyajit Ray's anti-war fantasy film

Goopi Gyne Bagha Byne. Released in 1969, the film depicts simpleton do-gooders Goopi and Bagha finding a purpose in life as their musical talents explode. In the climax sequence, they are shown evoking miraculous intervention by seeking earthen handis full of mishti as they make a final attempt to stop war between two princely states: Hallaa and Shundi.

The lyrics of the songs pay tribute to the quintessential Bengali sweetmeats (many of them home-made till date) like monda, mithai, mihidana, pulipithe, jibe goja, and more. On screen, the giant handis of sweetmeat drop from the sky as the warring men tumble over each other to get their fill!

THE 'GOOD FOOD' MAP OR WHAT EMERGED

Four decades into the twentieth century, World War II began and ended. The British in India were almost packing their bags. Their days were numbered, and India's independence was looking closer home. Calcutta was en masse involved in the freedom movement, with continuous political meets and rallies. Interestingly, the nationalist movement, a boastful reflection of Bengali participation towards nation-building, also became the fabric for searching identity, for seeking answers to 'Who are we?'

In the daily life of a middle-class Bengali of Calcutta, identity got mirrored through redefined 'our food', a cuisine that offered them a sense of belonging. However, 'our food' wasn't a wholistic idea; it was fragmented, conspicuous in its stratification of class, caste and religion resulting in an image of a Bengali self that had fine breakages. And yet, the Bengali middle class, in building their central cultural identity, was looking out for agencies that would help them blur these divides. To that, 'home' and proliferated restaurants, hotels, cha-er cabins, canteen, pice hotels and mishtir dokans, all got added.

The connotations of Bengalis as *khadya rashik* (connoisseur of food) with a sweet tooth, both epithets of self-fashioning, also emerged at this time. Food acted as leveller as they choose to frequent eateries and cafés like Indian Coffee House, Chachar Hotel, Shabir, New Alia, Basanta Cabin, Bijoli Grill, Café De Monico, Anadir Cabin, Golbari, Shyambazar, Nizam, Shiraz and Bhim Nag. This was Bengali cosmopolitanism—the result of colonial modernity. The choice to visit these 'hotels' (a peculiar colloquial term for any eatery outside home) meant the lines of 'who is the cook' and 'who is the eater' being blurred.

I would say this is more about all educated Bengalis in the urban context of Calcutta, where the composite nature of the palate was becoming the norm.

Thus, there would be omelettes, butter toasts with Polson butter, a glass of Horlicks, a Mughlai paratha, begun bhaja (fried slices of aubergine), chicken cutlets, fish fries, deemer devil (egg chops), telebhaja (deep-fried snacks), muri, mixed fried rice, pulao, biryani, stew, vegetable chop, jelly, pickles, mishti, cake, cha and coffee in loads, all included in amader khabar or our food at large. However random and radical this list may read, an amalgamated platter was what Bengalis of Calcutta were seeking on their plate. It was important to retain the 'Bengaliness' in their culinary and also to uphold the 'multicultural'. Therefore, a begun bhaja, cholar daal (thick daal made out of Bengal gram) and luchi could coexist with biryani, rezala, fish fry and rui macher quorma.

This coexistence formed the basis of how Bengalis would look at their traditional platter and the 'new food' relishing them together but not at home. Luchi, begun bhaja and cholar daal were home-made delights prepared by women, while biryani, rezala or cha with a fowl cutlet were surely to be had at hotels. Laced with these notions of *barir khabar* (home food) and *hotel-er khabar* (hotel food), the middle-class Bengalis of Calcutta set out to create new definitions of what must be their food. 'The narrative of Bengali cuisine is thus as much about the celebrations of domesticity and regional cosmopolitanism as about the fissure that helped in the self-fashioning of the Bengali middle-class,' writes Utsa Ray in *Culinary Culture in Colonial India.*[31]

By the 1950s, based on hotel-er khabar*,* a cartographic footprint of eatables emerged. They were gastronomic indicators, an endless trapeze of food routes created out of culinary desires, a way to navigate the city, much like present-day New York, which can be trailed through its cafés and eateries. Generational dwellers of colonial Calcutta went navigating the city through its bazaars and eateries, and not by historical monuments or parks, theatres, cinema halls and other cultural markers. Like a secret cryptographic code, it would not mean much for the unfamiliar; mere names of locations and eateries, but for those who sense Calcutta via its gastronomy, these are names of sinful drools and memories.

From north to south, with the nerve centre at Esplanade, the good food map emerged, expansive and myriad. The essence of these remembrances percolates into the present, reminding us of the hybridity of Bengali cuisine.

Shyambazar means its signature kosha mangsho of Golbari and chhanar jilipi of Adi Haridas Modak. Bidhan Sarani, Hatibagan for Chachar Hotel, which still serves Chacha's special fowl cutlet. They were the ones to introduce it. Close by stands the 100-year-old plus confectioner, Chittaranjan Mistanna Bhandar, famed for its madhuparka (flavoured yogurt), a word that originates in ancient Hindu texts described as a special offering of milk and honey.

Shobhabazaar, an adjacent locality, hosts a very old outlet of K.C. Das serving their legendary inventions roshogolla and rasmalai. The locality also has Sen Mahashay's knathal sandesh made with jackfruit centre-fill, which has been their original creation.

Jorabagan area is known for its 196-year-old confectioner Makhanlal Das, who came from Burdwan and became famous for his mishti doi and ratabi.

College Street would stand out for Indian Coffee House's strong cold coffee from days when a cup of coffee was priced at one crown, and was served with English weekly newspapers. Nearby, Paramount's daab (tender coconut) sherbet, green mango mania and keshar malai sherbets made of rabdi and milk have been quenching the city's thirst since 1918. The daab sherbet's recipe was scientist Prafulla Chandra Ray's invention, a coolant which he thought would help examinee students beat the harsh summer of Calcutta.

Dilkhusha Cabin stands not far away in their faded glory of kabiraji and their deemer devil from the original menu first served 122 years ago.

On Surya Sen Street is Kalika's telebhaja founded by freedom fighter Sukumar Datta. Telebhajas are the most tantalizing snacks. Till today, the man on the street would have his quick fill of muri and telebhajas. Smart and innovative, these savoury makers drew a lot from the bawarchis working for British residents, skillfully adopting the culture of snacks that the English enjoyed. Creditably, the local *telebhajar dokan* (shop selling deep-fried fritters) can deliver lip-smacking quick bites made from almost any ingredient including the most humble potato peel as well as green mango and pointed gourds.

The map would lead to Esplanade, a majestic encounter with all things Mughlai; the favourites being biryani, rezala, kathi rolls, pulao, Mutton Afghani, Chicken Arabi Halim, firni and shahi tukda—specialties spread across Aminia, Royal, Shabir, Nizam, Shiraz, New Alia and a bunch of eateries that began in the colonial era of the early 1900s.

There is no end to the culinary desirables that is the basis of this imagined food map. What needs to be noticed is the kind of food served in these eateries. Unquestionably, many of these dishes could not be prepared at home; hinderances were multiple, sometimes prohibition of ingredients, at other times, they needed a different skillset that only a bawarchi possessed.

However, most overwhelmingly, it was about *oder khabar* (the non-Hindu food) that lead to customization and measured acculturation. Although pioneering food writers such as Bipradas Mukhopadhyay and Pragyasundari Devi both made conscious efforts to introduce recipes with new fruits and vegetables as well as meats, in reality, social embargos limited them from being cooked at home. What got cooked at home was selective. Interestingly, dudha soup (milk soup, which had an egg yolk), a protein shake of present times, was permissible. Also, semui (vermicelli made from rice), a traditional pudding made and consumed during Islamic festivals like Eid, found a relatively easy entry. Bipradas Mukhopadhyay actually admired how semui, in Muslim homes, was finely cooked and recommended it for Hindu households too. Then there would be recipes like chicken diye pishpash, a prescribed nutritive diet for the ailing and kids.

While some were open to these experimentations, there

were others who were reluctant to give them a try. Instances of openness can be translated in tea parties of the affluent with Tayeb Alis and Hasan Butlers of the world serving fish fry, fowl cutlets and kebabs at home. For many, this would be a distant indulgence outside the fold of 'home'. Thus, the forbidden affair with hotel-er khabar began.

In the past, when pleasures of the 'outdoor' were unfamiliar to Calcutta of the late eighteenth century, it was the draw of taboo foods served at hotels like the Great Eastern and cabins like Chachar Hotel, which had a 'pied pipers' pull for men. This began to change around the time of the freedom movement, with many of the hotels transforming into hubs of dissent. The feisty Kobi Kazi Nazrul Islam spent hours at table number four of Favourite Cabin in College Street, where Subhas Chandra Bose would be his regular audience, listening to patriotic songs and poems.

The following decades of the 1950s and 1960s considered pleasures of the outdoors and eating out experiential, which meant social interactions and a welcome getaway from the routine. Eateries, too, expanded their scope, realigning themselves as trendy hubs, with students, poets, writers, artists, filmmakers and actors across gender and religion coming in droves, meeting and interacting. Hanging out at these places was interpreted as avant-garde and progressive.

Indian Coffee House and their likes had some customers visiting more than once a week, chatting for hours at the same table. To that, there were couples who carefully stayed away from prying eyes, meeting at these cabins and restaurants on their much-awaited dates. Invariably, food orders would be cutlets, kabirajis, kebabs, kathi rolls, parathas, fries, chops, boiled eggs, devils, toasts, omelettes and French fries infused with endless cups of piping hot tea and coffee.

The boundaries of Bengali consumption were pushed, easing up on what was so far tagged as 'forbidden'. With the advent of the educated younger generation, a range of popular, affordable cookbooks, lifestyle magazines publishing recipes and radio programme like *Mahila Mahal*, a new wave of inclusive cooking emerged. *Bhiyens* (make-shift kitchens or sweetmeat maker's temporary workstations at Bengali weddings) manned by *baro rannar thakur* (head Odia cook) and bawarchis and rakabdars hired for special occasions added to this changing milieu.

Soon, dishes like pulao, mutton quorma, Mutton Afghani, chicken jalfrezi, fish fry, mutton cutlets and biryanis were much desired in the menus of wedding. Animated discussions and family chatter around firming up of the final menu was a mini event in itself, with a head thakur or a bawarchi willing to display their culinary skills via trial servings.

In this extraordinary journey of tastes, habits, innovations, experiments, acceptance, indulgences, desires and celebrations, the final architect has been Calcutta. With its millions of khadya rashiks and the bhadraloks; British officials like Lord and Lady Canning; bazaars; the long list of European merchant entities like Lipton, Brooke Bond, Huntley Palmer, Polson Butter and others; Harmonic Tavern, Spence's Hotel and Great Eastern; the exiled ruler Nawab Wajid Ali Shah, his wazir Munshi ul-Sultan along with hundreds of bawarchis, rakabdars and khansamas; distinct entrepreneurs like Tong Achew, the Chinese businessman who introduced granulated sugar for the first time in Calcutta; bakers and confectioners like Federico Peletti, Angelo Firpo and John Richard; desi sweetmeat makers aka moiras; karigars as well as pioneers such as Nobin Chandra Das, Bhim Nag, Girish Chandra Dey and Nakul Chandra Nandy and many more who were passionately involved in the sweetish creations; the suppliers of raw ingredients including the classic *macher ardotdar* (the fish wholesaler) and finally generations of Bengali women—imaginative, talented and hard-working—and on occasions open to experimenting with new culinary ideas in the kitchen, it was only by 1970 that amader khabar underwent a major transformation, becoming liberal, turning over a new leaf.

Fifty-two years down the line, Calcutta happens to be equally insatiable in its appetite for delightful food and self-fashioning, letting the imagined map of 'good food' evolve, adding and erasing its gastronomic markers every now and then.

Acknowledgements

In a book that explores a story of food and happens to be the same foodstuff you have grown up eating, a note of thanks can be perplexing to write down.

A note of being indebted and thankful will go to many.

To that, I first thank innumerable shopkeepers and street-food vendors of Kolkata whom I have met over the years, who have made me cherish my first mutton rolls, a plate full of roadside hakka chow mein and those lip-smacking phuchkas (the Bengali version of the ever-popular panipuri). They made me curious about what Kolkata eats.

In these four years of writing, I have revisited many of them posing questions related to their craft. Within their cramped business hours, they had made time for me. Their answers became a repository of my invaluable field notes.

I am deeply grateful to Amitav Ghosh, one of the greatest authors of our times, for his kind words on this book and for taking out time to read the manuscript. Thank you,

Amitavda, I am beyond delighted.

My warmest thanks to Manzilat Fatima, the great-great-granddaughter of Nawab Wajid Ali Shah, who had generously shared her stories of Awadhi cuisine including recipes from her family, what she had learnt as a true Awadhi royal. She also made time from her busy chef hours demonstrating the unimaginably delicate, flavourful cuisine of Awadh–Lucknow, at her diner Manzilat's, exclusively for this book.

Thanks to all heritage confectioners of Kolkata: Bhim Chandra Nag, Girish Chandra Dey and Nakur Chandra Nandy, Putiram, Nabakrishna Guin, K.C. Das Grandsons, Sen Mahashay, and their current management for letting me and my colleague, photographer Irfan Nabi, to witness the exquisite art of sweet-making.

Many times I have been advised by Indrajit Chowdhury, an old colleague and historian from my *Anandabazar* days, on the research of eighteenth- and nineteenth-century Kolkata. Abhijit Sen, retired publication officer of Women's Studies Department, Jadavpur University, had shared unique information and leads related to the colonial era of Kolkata. I am thankful to them.

Libraries—Bangiyo Sahityo Parishat, Kolkata and the archives of the Centre for Studies in Social Sciences, Calcutta, have been integral to my work.

Thanks to Arun De, for sharing ephemeras like wedding menus and cards from the early 1900s and Rudra Banerjee, a friend and photographer, for sparing the time to manoeuvre the deep lanes of North Kolkata. Dr Anjum Rehman, for the ever-ongoing food discussions.

Over informal addas and phone conversations on Bengali food habits and culture that often lasted for hours, I have been enriched by inputs from my dear friend Tinni Mukherjee, my brother Sayantan Biswas and my beloved maternal grandmother Renu Ghosh Dastidar, an enthusiastic foodie and an energetic cook.

I have remembered my paternal grandmother more than once while working—a quiet, pensive personality, whose life was like that of a meditative culinary artist. She passed away when I was in school. But her memories of making magical home food all her life, never left me. She had taught me how to make pithe—a generic name for winter desserts popular in West Bengal and Bangladesh.

During the writing of this book, I lost my maternal grandmother, who had weaned me into my first eating out, the joy of savouring good food, and my foster mother, who was a very refined cook herself. I dedicate this book to these distinct women in my life and to my professor Subir Ray Chowdhury, who had first incited my love for colonial Kolkata many decades ago.

Extracts from *Lucknow: The Last Phase of an Oriental Culture* by Fakhir Hussain reproduced with permission of Oxford University Press India © Oxford University Press, 1989.

Notes

INTRODUCTION

1   A eulogy text on Goddess Chandi; it is a part of the group of Bengali religious texts titled *Mangal Kabyos*.

2   Rousselet, Louis, *India and Its Native Princes: Travels in Central India and in the Presidencies of Bombay and Bengal*, Bickers and Son, London, 1878, p. 602.

3   Ray, A.K., 'A Short History of Calcutta, Part I, Calcutta Towns and Suburbs', Chapter 1, *Census of India*, 1901, Volume VII, Bengal Secretariat Press, Calcutta, 1902, p. 4.

4   Ibid.11.

5   Wilson, C.R., *The Early Annals of the English in Bengal*, 'Chronology' segment, W. Thacker, London, 1895.

6   Ray, A.K., 'A Short History of Calcutta, Part I, Calcutta Towns and Suburbs', Chapter 3, *Census of India*, 1901, Volume VII, Bengal Secretariat Press, Calcutta, 1902, p. 11.

7   Wilson, C.R., *The Early Annals of the English in Bengal*, Chapter IV, p. 128, W. Thacker, London, 1895.

1. CHARNOCK, MUDDY TRACTS AND THE OLD COTTON MARKET

1. Ray, A.K., 'A Short History of Calcutta, Part I, Calcutta Towns and Suburbs', *Census of India*, 1901, Volume VII, Bengal Secretarial Press, Calcutta, 1902, p. 15.

2. Ibid.16.

3. Ibid.15.

4. Collingham, Lizzie, *Curry: A Tale of Cooks and Conquerors*, Vintage, London, 2005, p. 84.

5. Wilson, C.R., *The Early Annals of the English in Bengal*, Vol. I, W. Thacker, London, 1896, p. xvi.

6. Ibid.116.

7. Ibid.142.

8. William, Dalrymple, *The Anarchy: The East India Company, Corporate Violence, and The Pillage of an Empire*, Bloomsbury Publishing, London, 2019 p.25.

9. Collingham, Lizzie, *Curry: A Tale of Cooks and Conquerors*, Vintage, London, 2005, p. 86.

10. Ibid. 86.

11. William, Dalrymple, *The Anarchy: The East India Company Corporate Violence and the Pillage of an Empire*, Bloomsbury Publishing, London, 2019, pp. 25–26.

12. Ibid. 26.

13. Ray, A.K., 'A Short History of Calcutta, Volume VII, Calcutta Towns and Suburbs', *Census of India*, 1901, Bengal Secretarial Press, Calcutta, 1902, p. 17.

14. Basu, Shrimoyee, *Bazaars in the Changing Urban Space of Early Colonial Calcutta*, University of Calcutta, 2015, Chapter 6, p.13.

15. Wilson, C.R., *The Early Annals of the English in Bengal*, Vol. I, W. Thacker, London, 1896, p. 140.

16. Basu, Shrimoyee, *Bazaars in the Changing Urban Space of Early Colonial Calcutta*, University of Calcutta, 2015, Chapter 6, p.16.

17. Ray, A.K., 'A Short History of Calcutta, Volume VII, Calcutta: Towns and Suburbs', *Census of India*, 1901, Bengal Secretarial Press, Calcutta, 1902, p. 21.

18. Ibid. 24.

19. bid. 26-27.

20. Ibid. 22, 23.

21. Keay, John, *India Discovered: The Achievement of the British Raj*, Windward, London, 1981, p. 21.

22. Dalrymple, William, *The Anarchy: The East India Company, Corporate Violence, and the Pillage of an Empire*, Bloomsbury Publishing, London, 2019, p. 70.

23. Basu, Shrimoyee, *Bazaars in the Changing Urban Space of Early Colonial Calcutta*, University of Calcutta, 2015, p. 30.

24. Ibid. 30.

25. Ibid. 25.

26. Ray, A.K., 'A Short History of Calcutta, Volume VII, Calcutta: Towns and Suburbs', *Census of India*, 1901, Bengal Secretarial Press, Calcutta, 1902, p. 11.

27. Ibid. 11.

28. Dalrymple, William, *The Anarchy:The East India Company, Corporate Violence, and the Pillage of an Empire*, Bloomsbury Publishing, London, 2019, p. 71.

29. Ibid. 25.

30. Ibid. 70.

31. Ibid. 74.

32. Ibid. 71.

33. Brennan, Jennifer, *Curries & Bugles: A Memoir & Cookbook of the British Raj*, Viking, Penguin Books, USA, 1990, p. 9.

34. Yule, Sir Henry and Arthur Coke Burnell, *Hobson-Jobson:*

A Dictionary of Colloquial Words and Phrases, John Murray, London, 1903, Introductory Remark, p. xv.

35. Ibid. xviii.

36. Collingham, Lizzie, *Curry: A Tale of Cooks and Conquerors*, Vintage, Great Britain, 2006, Chapter 6, p.138.

37. Carey, W.H., *The Good Old Days of Honorable John Company*, Calcutta Quins Book Co., 1882, Riddhi Edition, Calcutta, 1980, Chapter xi, p. 74.

38. Bahadur, John Barleycorn, *Old Time Taverns in India*, H. Hobbes Thacker, Spink & Co., Calcutta, 1944, Chapter: 'Calcutta Taverns', p. 142.

39. Ray, Bharati (ed.), *Collected Volumes Bamabodhini Patrika (1270-1339 Bangadda)*, Pustak Biponi, Calcutta, 1999, pp.114-17.

2. 'TURTLES DRESSED, GENTLEMEN BOARDED'

1. Long, Reverend Father James, *Calcutta and Its Neighbourhood: History of People and Localities from 1690 to 1857*, Indian Publications, Calcutta, 1974, p. 98.

2. Dalrymple, William, *The Anarchy: The East India Company, Corporate Violence, and the Pillage of an Empire*, pp. 314-15, Bloomsbury Publishing, London, 2019.

3. Hickman, Katie, *She Merchants, Buccaneers & Gentlewomen: British Women in India*, Virago Press, USA, 2019, p. 76.

4. Ibid.76.

5. Ray, A.K., 'A Short History of Calcutta', *Census of India,* 1901, Volume VII (Calcutta: Town and suburbs), Bengal Secretarial Press, Calcutta, 1902, pp. 97-98.

6. Basu, Shrimoyee, *Bazaars in the Changing Urban Space of Early Colonial Calcutta*, University of Calcutta, 2015, p. 36.

7. Ibid. 44.

8. Carey, W.H., *The Good Old Days of Honourable John Company*,

Calcutta Quins Book Co, 1882, Riddhi Edition, Calcutta, 1944, Chapter XI, p. 182.

9. Ibid.176.

10. Ibid.191.

11. Ibid.176.

12. Ibid.193.

13. Ibid.194.

14. Borthwick, Meredith, *Shadow or Substance: The Changing Role of Women in Bengal, 1849-1905,* Australian National University, Thesis, 1980, p. 64.

15. Ibid. 66.

16. Ibid. 226.

17. Ibid. 227.

18. Sarkar, Tanika, *Hindu Wife, Hindu Nation: Community, Religion, and Cultural Nationalism*, Permanent Black, Ranikhet, 2001, p. 38.

19. Collingham, Lizzie, *Curry: A Tale of Cooks and Conquerors*, Vintage, London, 2006, Chapter 6, p.111.

20. Ibid.107.

21. Kincaid, Dennis, *British Social Life in India*, Rupa Publications, New Delhi, 2015, p.113.

22. Collingham, Lizzie, *Curry: A Tale of Cooks and Conquerors*, Vintage, London, 2006, Chapter 6, p.111.

23. Dalrymple, William, *The Anarchy: The East India Company, Corporate Violence, and the Pillage of an Empire*, Bloomsbury Publishing, London, 2019, p. 315.

24. Ray, A.K., 'A Short History of Calcutta', *Census of India,*1901, Volume VII (Calcutta: Town and suburbs), Bengal Secretarial Press, Calcutta, 1902, p. 51.

25. Ibid. 48.

26. Collingham Lizzie, *Curry: A Tale of Cooks and Conquerors*, Vintage, London, 2006, Chapter 6, p.112.

27. Ibid.112-13.

28. Fay, Eliza et al., *The Original Letters from India of Mrs. Eliza Fay*, Thacker, Spink and Co., Calcutta, 1908, p. 140.

29. Kincaid, Dennis, *British Social Life in India,* Rupa Publications, New Delhi, 2015, p.120.

30. Ray, Utsa, *Culture of Food in Colonial Bengal*, University of Pennsylvania, 2009, p. 14.

31. Collingham, Lizzie, *Curry: A Tale of Cooks and Conquerors*, Vintage, London, 2006, Chapter 6, p.180.

32. Belnos, Sophie Charlotte, *Twenty-Four Plates Illustrative of Hindoo and European Manners in Bengal Drawn on Stone by A. Collin from the Sketches of Mrs. Belnos*, Smith Elder Cornhill, London, 1832.

33. Nevile, Pran, *Nautch Girls of the Raj*, Penguin Books India, India, 2009 p. 36.

34. Ibid. 34-35.

35. Tschirky, Oscar, *Oscar of the Waldorf's Cookbook*, The Werner Company, New York, 1896, p. v, p. vi.

36. Sengupta, Jayanta, *Nation on a Platter: The Culture and Politics of Food and Cuisine in Colonial Bengal*, Cambridge University Press (online publication), 2009, p. 85.

37. Anglo Indian, *Indian Outfits and Establishments: Practical Guide for Persons About to reside in India; Detailing the Articles Which Should Be Taken Out, and the Requirements of Home Life and Management There*, L. Upcott Gill, London, 1882, p. 86.

38. Ibid. 85.

39. Bahadur John Barleycorn, *Old Time Taverns in India*, Thacker, Spink & Co, Calcutta, 1944, p. 123.

40. Ibid.111.

41. Ibid.112.

42. Ray, Utsa, *Culinary Culture in Colonial India: A Cosmopolitan*

Platter and the Middle-Class, Cambridge University Press, New Delhi, 2015, p. 56.

43. Ibid. 17.

44. Ibid.

45. Ray, Utsa, Culture of Food in Colonial Bengal, University of Pennsylvania, 2009, p. 144.

46. Bahadur, John Barleycorn, Old Time Taverns in India, Thacker, Spink & Co., Calcutta, 1944, pp. 49-50.

47. William, Arnold Delafield, Oakfield: Or, the Fellowship in the East, Longman, London, 1853, p. 212.

48. Yule, Henry, Sir, Hobson-Jobson: A Glossary of Colloquial Anglo-Indian Words and Phrases, and of Kindred Terms, Etymological, Historical, Geographical and Discursive, John Murray, London, 1903 p.129.

49. Collingham, Lizzie, Curry: A Tale of Cooks and Conquerors, Vintage, London, 2009, pp. 122–23.

50. Bahadur, John Barleycorn, Old Time Taverns in India, Thacker, Spink & Co., Calcutta, 1944, pp. 50-51.

51. Collingham, Lizzie, Curry: A Tale of Cooks and Conquerors, Vintage, London, 2009, p.124.

52. Ibid. 125.

53. Ibid.123.

54. From the Hooghly to the Himalayas: Being an Illustrated Handbook to the Chief Places of Interest Reached by the Eastern Bengal State Railway, Eastern Bengal State Railway, 1913, p. 15.

55. Ibid.

56. https://bit.ly/3Pt8HjL, accessed on 23 July 2022.

57. Ray, Utsa, Culinary Culture in Colonial India: A Cosmopolitan Platter and the Middle-Class, Cambridge University Press, New Delhi, 2015, p. 58.

58. Sharar, Abdul Halim, Lucknow: The Last Phase of an Oriental

Culture, Translated and edited by E.S. Harcourt and Fakhir Hussain, OUP, New Delhi, India edition, 1989, p. 75.

59. Ibid. 74.

60. Ibid. 63.

61. Ibid. 65.

62. Collingham, Lizzie, *Curry: A Tale of Cooks and Conquerors*, Vintage, London, 2009, p. 28.

63. Ibid. 30.

64. Sharar, Abdul Halim, *Lucknow: The Last Phase of an Oriental Culture*, Translated and edited by E.S. Harcourt and Fakhir Hussain, OUP, New Delhi, India edition 1989, p. 155.

65. Ibid.156.

66. Ibid. 159.

67. Collingham, Lizzie, *Curry: A Tale of Cooks and Conquerors*, Vintage, London, 2009, p. 27.

68. Ray Utsa, *Culture of Food in Colonial Bengal,* University of Pennsylvania, 2009, pp. 54-55.

69. Ibid. 178.

70. Sharar, Abdul Halim, *Lucknow: The Last Phase of an Oriental Culture*, Translated and edited by E.S. Harcourt and Fakhir Hussain, OUP, New Delhi, India edition, 1989, p. 70.

71. Collingham, Lizzie, *Curry: A Tale of Cooks and Conquerors*, Vintage, 2009, p. 95.

72. Sharar, Abdul Halim, *Lucknow: The Last Phase of an Oriental Culture*, Translated and edited by E.S. Harcourt and Fakhir Hussain, OUP, New Delhi, India edition, 1989, pp. 157–58.

73. Ibid.162.

74. Ibid.160.

75. Collingham, Lizzie, *Curry: A Tale of Cooks and Conquerors*, Vintage, London, 2009, pp. 93-94.

76. Sharar, Abdul Halim, *Lucknow: The Last Phase of an Oriental*

Culture, Translated and edited by E.S. Harcourt and Fakhir Hussain, OUP, New Delhi, India edition, 1989, p. 167.

77. Bahadur, John Barleycorn, *Old Time Taverns in India*, Thacker, Spink & Co., Calcutta, 1944, pp. 142–43.

78. Wyvern, *Culinary Jottings*, Higginbotham and Co., 1885, p. 177.

79. Ibid.178.

80. Collingham, Lizzie, *Curry: A Tale of Cooks and Conquerors*,Vintage, London, 2009, p.183.

81. Chakrabarti, Gautam, 'Fowl-Cutlets and Mutton Singāḍās: Intercultural Food and Cuisine/s in Bengali Detective Fiction', *A World of Nourishment: Reflections on Food in Indian Culture*, Cinzia Pieruccini and Paola M. Rossi (eds), Ledizioni, Milan, 2016.

3. GUAVA JELLY, OR THE GOOD HOUSEKEEPER CODE

1. Ray, Utsa, *Culinary Culture in Colonial India: A Cosmopolitan Platter and the Middle-Class*, Cambridge University Press, New Delhi, 2015, p.146.

2. Borthwick, Meredith, *Shadow or Substance: The Changing Role of Women in Bengal, 1849-1905*, Australian National University, 1980, p. 227.

3. Ibid. 218.

4. Basu, Priyanath, *Grihadharmma*, Calcutta, 1936, p. 50.

5. Ibid.

6. Ray, Utsa, *Culinary Culture in Colonial India: A Cosmopolitan Platter and the Middle-Class*, Cambridge University Press, New Delhi, 2015, p. 231.

7. Cited in Sarkar, Tanika, *Hindu Wife, Hindu Nation: Community, Religion and Cultural Nationalism*, Permanent Black, Ranikhet, 2001 p. 95.

8. Ibid. 95.

9. Ibid. 121.

10. A eulogy literature of the medieval Bhakti movement leader and reformist Chaitanya Dev (1486-1534), who was also a proponent of Vaishnavism in Bengal.

11. Borthwick, Meredith, *Shadow or Substance: The Changing Role of Women in Bengal, 1849-1905*, Australian National University, 1980, pp.84-85.

12. Ibid. 85.

13. Ibid. 226.

14. Ray, Utsa, *Culinary Culture in Colonial India: A Cosmopolitan Platter and the Middle-Class*, Cambridge University Press, New Delhi, 2015, pp.110-11.

15. Borthwick, Meredith, *Shadow or Substance: The Changing Role of Women in Bengal, 1849-1905*, Australian National University, 1980, pp. 84-85.

16. *Bamabodhini Patrika,* October 1882, *Collected Anthology of Essays: Nari O Paribar, Bamabodhini Patrika (1270-1329 Bangabda),* Bharati Ray (ed.), Pustak Biponi, Kolkata, 1999.

17. Chakraborty, Punyalata, *Chelebelar Dinguli*, New Script, 1958, p. 97.

18. Ibid. 98.

19. Ibid. 4-5.

20. Borthwick, Meredith, *Shadow or Substance: The Changing Role of Women in Bengal, 1849-1905*, Australian National University, 1980, p.79.

21. Chakraborty, Punyalata, *Chelebelar Dinguli*, New Script, Calcutta, 1958, p.17.

22. Guha-Thakurta, Tapati, *The City in the Archive: Calcutta's Visual Histories,* Centre for Studies in Social Sciences, Calcutta, 2011, p. 34.

23. Appadurai, Arjun, *How to Make a National Cuisine: Cookbooks in Contemporary India*, University of Pennsylvania, Cambridge University Press (online edition), 2009, p.1.

24. Gupta, Abhijit, 'Royal Recipes', https://bit.ly/3SmBNU5, accessed on 5 August 2022.

25. Borthwick, Meredith, *Shadow or Substance: The Changing Role of Women in Bengal, 1849-1905*, Australian National University, 1980, p. 228.

26. Mukhopadhyay, Bipradas, *Pak Pranali*, Vol 1-5 (Fifth Edition), Haridas and Gurudas Chattopadhyay, Calcutta, 1906, pp. 29–31.

27. Borthwick, Meredith, *Shadow or Substance: The Changing Role of Women in Bengal, 1849-1905,* Australian National University, 1980, p. 18.

28. Ibid. 219.

29. Mukhopadhyay, Bipradas, *Pak Pranali*, Vol 1-5 (Fifth Edition), Haridas and Gurudas Chattopadhyay, Calcutta, 1906, pp. 30–31.

30. Ibid.161.

31. Ray, Utsa, *Culinary Culture in Colonial India: A Cosmopolitan Platter and the Middle-Class*, Cambridge University Press, New Delhi, 2015, p. 63.

32. Borthwick, Meredith, *Shadow or Substance: The Changing Role of Women in Bengal, 1849-1905*,Australian National University,1980, p. 228.

33. Ibid. 228.

34. Ray, Utsa, *Culinary Culture in Colonial India: A Cosmopolitan Platter and the Middle-Class*, Cambridge University Press, New Delhi, 2015 p. 64.

35. Ibid. 45.

36. Ibid. 42-43.

37. *Punya,* Volume 1, Archives, Centre for Social Sciences Kolkata, 1897, p. 18.

38. *Punya,* Volume 2, Archives, Centre for Social Sciences Kolkata, 1897, p. 76-82.

39. Devi, Pragyasundari, *Amish O Niramish*, Vol.1 (Eighth edition, 2017), Ananda Publishers, Kolkata, 1990, p. 53.

40. Ibid.

41. Ibid; Second edition advertisement, Pragyasundari Devi, *Amish O Niramish*, Vol.1, Eighth ed. 2017, Ananda Publishers, Kolkata, 1990.

42. Ibid. 102, 114 and 442.

43. *Antahpur,* Volume 4, Issue 1, p.14, Issue 9, p. 214, 1901, Archives, Centre for Social Sciences Kolkata.

44. Das, Rituparna, 'Reading Women Through Their Recipes', *Sahapedia.org*, September 2021, https://bit.ly/3PVXmsD, accessed on 25 July 2022.

45. Ibid.

46. Ray, Utsa, *Culinary Culture in Colonial India: A Cosmopolitan Platter and the Middle-Class*, Cambridge University Press, New Delhi, 2015, p. 69.

47. Chaudhurani, Renuka Devi, *Rakamari Amish Ranna*, Ananda Publishers, Kolkata, 2003, Eighth edition.

48. Ray, Utsa, *Culinary Culture in Colonial India: A Cosmopolitan Platter and the Middle-Class*, Cambridge University Press, New Delhi, 2015, p. 74.

49. Mazumder, Mukhopadhyay, Leela, *Shahasro Ek Ranna*, Mahesh Publication, Calcutta, 1990.

50. Chakrabarti, Gautam, 'Fowl-Cutlets and Mutton Siṅgāḍās: Intercultural Food and Cuisine/s in Bengali Detective Fiction', pp. 308–09, *A World of Nourishment: Reflections on Food in Indian Culture*, Cinzia Pieruccini and Paola M. Rossi (eds), Ledizioni, Milan, 2016.

51. Ibid. 307.

52. Mukherjee, Tilottama, 'The Co-Ordinating State and the Economy: The Nizamat in Eighteenth-Century Bengal', *Modern Asian Studies,* Vol. 43, No. 2 (March 2009), pp. 389-436, Cambridge University Press (online publication).

53. Hussein Khan Tabatabai, Syed Gholam, *Seir Mutaqherin*, R. Cambray and Co. Calcutta, Vol. II, pp. 156-57.

54. Ibid.157.

55. Mukherjee, Tilottama, 'The Co-Ordinating State and the Economy: The Nizamat in Eighteenth-Century Bengal', *Modern Asian Studies,* Vol. 43, No. 2 (March 2009), pp. 389-436, Cambridge University Press (online publication).

56. Ibid. 108, 410.

57. Collingham, Lizzie, *Curry: A Tale of Cooks and Conquerors,* Vintage, London, 2009, p.195.

58. Ibid.191.

59. Chakraborty, Punyalata, *Chelebelar Dinguli*, New Script, Calcutta, 1958, p.4, p. 73.

60. Bhadra, Gautam, *From an Imperial Product to a National Drink: The Culture of Tea Consumption in Modern India*, Centre for Social Sciences, Calcutta, 2005, p.8.

61. Sanyal, Amitava, 'Mahatma Gandhi and His Anti-Tea Campaign', BBC, 7 May 2012, https://bbc.in/3PUtj4t, accessed on 26 July 2022.

62. Bhadra, Gautam, *From an Imperial Product to a National Drink: The Culture of Tea Consumption in Modern India*, Centre for Social Sciences, 2005, p. 14.

63. Ibid. 15.

64. Collingham, Lizzie, *Curry: A Tale of Cooks and Conquerors,* Vintage, London, 2009, p.196.

65. Ibid.

66. Ibid.194.

67. Bhadra, Gautam, *From an Imperial Product to a National Drink; The Culture of Tea Consumption in Modern India*, Centre for Social Sciences in association with Tea Board, 2005, p.12.

68. Ibid. 16-17.

69. Chakrabarti, Gautam, 'Fowl-Cutlets and Mutton Singāḍās: Intercultural Food and cuisine/s in Bengali detective fiction', p. 308, *A World of Nourishment: Reflections on Food in Indian Culture*, Cinzia Pieruccini and Paola M. Rossi (eds), Ledizioni, Milan, 2016.

70. Guha-Thakurta, Tapati, *The City in the Archive*, Calcutta's Visual Histories, CSSSC/Seagull Arts & Media Resource Centre, Calcutta, 2011, p. 35.

4. TANGERINE REALITIES

1. Ray, Utsa, *Culinary Culture in Colonial India: A Cosmopolitan Platter and the Middle-Class*, Cambridge University Press, New Delhi, 2015, p.108.

2. Ibid.

3. Borthwick, Meredith, *Shadow or Substance: The Changing Role of Women in Bengal, 1849-1905*, Australian National University, 1980, p.111.

4. Ibid. 103.

5. Bose, Shib Chunder, *The Hindoos As They Are: A Description of Manners, Customs and Inner Life of Hindu Society in Bengal,* Thacker Spink & Co., London, Second edition, 1883.

6. Ibid.115.

7. Mukhopadhyay, Jogendra, 'Shekaler Bibaha', *Prabasi*, Volume 1, Baishakh, 1345 (1938), p. 29.

8. Deb, Chitra, *Thakurbarir Andarmahal*, Ananda Publishers, Kolkata, 1952, p.78.

9. Ray, Utsa, *Culinary Culture in Colonial India: A Cosmopolitan*

Platter and the Middle-Class, Cambridge University Press, New Delhi, 2015, p.117.

10. Ibid. 74-75.

11. Acharya, K.T., *A Historical Dictionary of Indian Food*, OUP, New Delhi, 1998, p.180.

12. Banerji, Chitrita, *The Hour of the Goddess: Memories of Women Food and Ritual in Bengal*, Seagull-Penguin Random House India, India, 2006, p. 110.

13. Ibid.111.

14. Ibid.112.

15. Firminger, Rev. W.K., *Thacker's Guide to Calcutta*, Thacker & Spink, Calcutta, 1906, p. 5.

16. Translated by the author himself from the original Bengali *Bhojon-shilpi Bangali.* The translation has been published in the daily newspaper *The Hindusthan Standard* of Calcutta. The Bangla article, first titled 'Bhojan-Bilasi Bangali', but later changed to 'Bhojon-shilpi Bangali', appeared in four daily installments in the *Anandabazar Patrika* of Calcutta, during 1-4 January 1971.

17. Acharya, K.T., *A Historical Dictionary of Indian Food*, OUP, New Delhi, 1998, p.157.

18. Acharya, K.T., *Indian Food: A Historical Companion*, OUP, New Delhi, 1994, p. 91.

19. Banerji, Chitrita, *The Hour of the Goddess: Memories of Women Food and Ritual in Bengal*, Seagull-Penguin Random House India, 2006, p. 118.

20. Acharya, K.T., *Indian Food: A Historical Companion*, OUP, New Delhi, 1994, p. 62.

21. Acharya, K.T., *A Historical Dictionary of Indian Food*, OUP, New Delhi, 1998, p. 23.

22. Sanger, Satya Prakash, *Food and Drinks in Mughal India*, Reliance Publishing House, New Delhi, 1999, p. 42.

23. Krondl, Michael, 'The Sweetshops of Kolkata', *Gastronomica,* Vol. 10, No. 3 (Summer 2010), pp. 58-65, California University Press.

24. Acharya K.T., *A Historical Dictionary of Indian Food*, OUP, New Delhi, 1998, p. 23.

25. It is a traditional unit of mass calculation in British era. Approximately 37.72 kilograms equals to 1 maund.

26. Debi, Saradsundari, *Phire Dekha,* Volume 2, 1913; Repr., Kolkata Subarnarekha, 2010, pp. 3-5.

27. Bose, Shib Chunder, *The Hindoos As They Are: A Description of Manners, Customs and Inner Life of Hindu Society in Bengal* (Second edition) p. 51, p. 116, Thacker Spink & Co., London, 1883, p. 24.

28. Ibid. 51.

29. Ibid.103.

30. Krondl, Michael, 'The Sweetshops of Kolkata', *Gastronomica,* Vol. 10, No. 3 (Summer 2010), pp. 58-65, California University Press.

31. Ray, Utsa, *Culinary Culture in Colonial India: A Cosmopolitan Platter and the Middle-Class*, Cambridge University Press, New Delhi, 2015, p.105.

Printed in Great Britain
by Amazon

15040097R00119